Betty Crocker's

RED SPOON COLLECTION™

BEST RECIPES FOR
COOKIES

PRENTICE HALL PRESS

New York   London   Toronto   Sydney   Tokyo

Published by Prentice Hall Press
A Division of Simon & Schuster, Inc.
15 Columbus Circle
New York, NY 10023

Published simultaneously in Canada by
Prentice Hall Canada Inc.

PRENTICE HALL PRESS is a registered
trademark of Simon & Schuster, Inc.

BETTY CROCKER is a registered trademark of
General Mills, Inc.

RED SPOON COLLECTION is a trademark of
General Mills, Inc.

Library of Congress Cataloging-in-Publication

Betty Crocker's Red Spoon collection. Cookies.
p.   cm.
Includes index.
ISBN 0-13-073073-4 : $9.95
1. Cookies.
TX772.B54 1989
641.8'654—dc 19   88-26588
CIP

Manufactured in the United States of America

10 9 8 7 6 5 4 3

CONTENTS

INTRODUCTION

Cookies

What is more enticing than the aroma of cookies baking? Homemade cookies are so many things: instant comfort, great after-school treats, rustic take-along desserts or truly satisfying morsels. There is something special about cookies. A basket or tin of cookies makes a delectable gift that never fails to delight. Baking cookies can inspire a reflective mood when done alone and is all the more fun when done with a friend. And it is an ideal introduction to the kitchen, whether the first-time baker works at grandmother's side or in brave solitude. You simply can't have *too many* cookies in the house, and that's just what this book is all about.

Baking Cookies

Before you roll up your sleeves and start mixing cookie dough, read the recipe through carefully. Nothing is more irritating than discovering that you need to make another trip to the store to fetch a critical ingredient. Be sure to assemble the equipment you need before you start. You probably have most of the necessary utensils (baking cookies calls for nothing very so-

phisticated in the way of equipment), but it is reassuring to know you have everything conveniently at hand.

Rules

The key to successful baking is adhering to a number of rules:

- Follow the recipe exactly, measuring the ingredients accurately.
- To ensure uniform baking, make all the cookies in one batch the same size.
- Follow directions for greasing (or greasing and flouring) baking sheets and pans.
- Allow the oven to heat to the temperature called for in the recipe.
- Use shiny cookie sheets rather than black steel ones. The black steel sheets speed browning on the bottom surface but frequently overbrown the bottom of quick-baking goods, such as cookies, and leave the rest of the cookie underdone.
- Bake one sheet of cookies at a time and position it on the center oven rack. Use a cookie sheet two inches shorter and narrower than the interior of your oven, so that hot air can circulate for even baking. If you must use two sheets, space

them so that one is not directly over the other and switch the positions of the sheets halfway through the baking time.

- Always place dough on a cool cookie sheet. Dough spreads on a hot one, and this can be disastrous if you are making specially shaped cookies.
- Check at the end of the minimum baking time to see if the cookies are done. No two ovens bake quite the same way, and baking times are only approximate. If the cookies aren't done when you check them, you can bake them longer; overdone cookies simply stay that way.

Measuring Correctly

It is important to remember when baking cookies to measure all ingredients correctly. The following is a list of hints for measuring:

- Dry ingredients: Scoop your measure (graduated measuring spoon or graduated measuring cup) full, then level by passing a straight edge evenly across the rim of the measure.
- Liquid ingredients: Pour into a liquid measuring cup, then read the measurement at eye level. It's best to set the measure on a level surface and bend down to read it, because it's nearly impossible to hold it perfectly still in front of you.
- Measure the following with special care:

    Brown sugar, fats and shortening should be spooned into a graduated measure and packed down firmly.

    Flour should not be sifted before measuring unless the recipe directs otherwise.

Measure powdered sugar and variety baking mix by spooning lightly into a cup, then leveling as when measuring any other dry ingredient. Sift powdered sugar only if it is lumpy.

Nuts, coconut and chopped or dried fruit may be packed down lightly when measured.

Storing Cookies

Thin, crisp cookies can be kept loosely covered. If they lose their crispness, warm them at 300° for three to five minutes. Soft or chewy cookies should be kept tightly covered. If they show a tendency to dry out, place a slice of apple or fresh bread in the container with them (don't forget to replace the apple or bread every few days).

Cookie Clinic

If your cookie dough seems very dry and difficult to handle, add one or two tablespoons of cream or milk. If it is too soft to shape or roll, mix in one or two tablespoons of flour. Do not overmix dough after flour has been added, or the cookies will be tough. Remember: Follow the recipe exactly.

Even with all of these hints, you will want to refer from time to time to the Red Spoon Tips section (page 97). There you will find a detailed discussion of the ingredients used in baking these cookies and how to make substitutions; how to freeze cookies; which cookies travel well (and how to pack them to ensure minimum breakage); cookie "menus" for holidays, tea parties and bake sales; decorating tips, and much more.

THE BETTY CROCKER EDITORS

BAR COOKIES

Snowy Apricot Bars

75 BARS

*1 package (6 ounces) dried apricots
  (1 1/3 cups)*
1/2 cup firm margarine or butter
1/2 cup granulated sugar
2 1/2 cups variety baking mix
2 cups packed brown sugar
4 eggs, beaten
2/3 cup variety baking mix
1 teaspoon vanilla
1 cup chopped nuts
Powdered sugar

Place apricots in 2-quart saucepan; add enough water to cover. Heat to boiling; reduce heat. Simmer uncovered 10 minutes; drain. Cool; chop and reserve.

Heat oven to 350°. Cut margarine into granulated sugar and 2 1/2 cups baking mix. Pat in ungreased jelly roll pan, 15 1/2 × 10 1/2 × 1 inch. Bake until light brown, about 10 minutes.

Beat brown sugar and eggs. Stir in apricots, 2/3 cup baking mix, the vanilla and nuts. Spread over baked layer. Bake 30 minutes longer. Cool completely; sprinkle with powdered sugar. Cut into bars, about 2 × 1 inch.

Following pages: **From left to right:** *Snowy Apricot Bars, Spicy Toffee Triangles and Caramel-Apple Bars*

Caramel-Apple Bars

36 BARS

1 cup packed brown sugar
1/2 cup margarine or butter, softened
1/4 cup shortening
1 3/4 cups all-purpose flour
1 1/2 cups quick-cooking oats
1 teaspoon salt
1/2 teaspoon baking soda
4 1/2 cups coarsely chopped pared tart apples (about 3 medium)
3 tablespoons all-purpose flour
1 package (14 ounces) caramel candies

Heat oven to 400°. Mix brown sugar, margarine and shortening. Stir in 1 3/4 cups flour, the oats, salt and baking soda. Remove 2 cups of the mixture; reserve. Press remaining mixture in ungreased rectangular pan, 13 × 9 × 2 inches.

Toss apples and 3 tablespoons flour; spread over mixture in pan. Heat candies over low heat, stirring occasionally, until melted; pour evenly over apples. Top with reserved oat mixture; press lightly.

Bake until golden brown and apples are tender, 25 to 30 minutes. Cut into bars, about 2 × 1 1/2 inches, while warm. Refrigerate any remaining bars.

Almond-Meringue Shortbreads

36 SQUARES

2 cups all-purpose flour
2 eggs, separated
1/2 cup sugar
1/4 teaspoon salt
3/4 cup margarine or butter, softened
1/2 cup chopped slivered almonds
1/2 cup raspberry or strawberry jam or jelly
1/3 cup sugar
1/2 cup slivered almonds

Heat oven to 400°. Mix flour, egg yolks, 1/2 cup sugar, the salt, margarine and 1/2 cup chopped almonds (dough will be very stiff). Press dough in ungreased square pan, 9 × 9 × 2 inches. Bake until edges are light brown, 15 to 20 minutes; cool slightly. Spread with jam.

Beat egg whites until foamy. Beat in 1/3 cup sugar gradually; continue beating until stiff and glossy. Spread meringue over jam; sprinkle with 1/2 cup slivered almonds. Bake until meringue is light brown, 8 to 10 minutes. Cool slightly; cut into about 1 1/2-inch squares.

Toffee Bars

1 cup packed brown sugar
1 cup margarine or butter, softened
1 teaspoon vanilla
1 egg yolk
2 cups all-purpose flour
1/4 teaspoon salt
1 bar (4 ounces) milk chocolate candy
1/2 cup chopped nuts

Heat oven to 350°. Mix brown sugar, margarine, vanilla and egg yolk. Stir in flour and salt. Press in greased rectangular pan, 13 × 9 × 2 inches.

Bake until very light brown, 25 to 30 minutes (crust will be soft). Immediately place separated pieces of chocolate candy on crust. Let stand until soft; spread evenly. Sprinkle with nuts. Cut into bars, about 2 × 1½ inches, while warm.

Spicy Toffee Triangles

1 cup packed brown sugar
1 cup margarine or butter, softened
1 egg, separated
1 teaspoon vanilla
2 cups all-purpose flour
1/4 teaspoon salt
1 teaspoon ground cinnamon
1 cup chopped walnuts

Heat oven to 275°. Mix brown sugar, margarine, egg yolk and vanilla. Stir in flour, salt and cinnamon. Spread in ungreased jelly roll pan, 15½ × 10½ × 1 inch. Brush dough with unbeaten egg white. Sprinkle with walnuts; press lightly. Bake 1 hour. While warm, cut into 2½-inch squares, then cut each square diagonally into halves; cool.

GREEK TRIANGLES: Substitute ground cardamom for the cinnamon and 1 can (5 ounces) diced roasted almonds for the walnuts.

HAWAIIAN SPICE TRIANGLES: Substitute ground ginger for the cinnamon and ¼ cup chopped salted macadamia nuts and ¼ cup flaked coconut for the walnuts.

Date Bars

Date Filling (below)
1 cup packed brown sugar
½ cup margarine or butter, softened
¼ cup shortening
1¾ cups all-purpose or whole wheat
   flour
1 teaspoon salt
½ teaspoon baking soda
1½ cups quick-cooking oats

Prepare Date Filling; cool. Heat oven to 400°. Mix brown sugar, margarine and shortening. Stir in remaining ingredients. Press half of the crumbly mixture in greased baking pan, 13 × 9 × 2 inches; spread with filling. Top with remaining crumbly mixture; press lightly. Bake until light brown, 25 to 30 minutes. Cut into bars, 2 × 1 inch, while warm.

DATE FILLING

1 package (16 ounces) dates, cut up
   (about 3 cups)
1½ cups water
¼ cup sugar

Mix dates, water and sugar in saucepan. Cook over low heat, stirring constantly, until thickened, about 10 minutes.

Date-Nut Squares

2 eggs
½ cup sugar
½ teaspoon vanilla
½ cup all-purpose flour
½ teaspoon baking powder
½ teaspoon salt
2 cups cut-up dates
1 cup chopped nuts

Heat oven to 350°. Grease a baking pan, 9 × 9 × 2 inches. Beat eggs until light and lemon colored. Beat in sugar and vanilla thoroughly. Blend in flour, baking powder and salt, then stir in dates and nuts. Spread in the pan.

Bake 25 to 30 minutes. Cool and cut into squares. Roll the squares in powdered sugar, if desired.

Pumpkin Spice Bars

4 eggs
2 cups sugar
1 cup vegetable oil
1 can (16 ounces) pumpkin
2 cups all-purpose flour
2 teaspoons baking powder
2 teaspoons ground cinnamon
1 teaspoon baking soda
3/4 teaspoon salt
1/2 teaspoon ground ginger
1/4 teaspoon ground cloves
1/2 cup raisins
Cream Cheese Frosting (below)
1/2 cup chopped nuts

Heat oven to 350°. Grease jelly roll pan, 15 1/2 × 10 1/2 × 1 inch. Beat eggs, sugar, oil and pumpkin. Stir in flour, baking powder, cinnamon, baking soda, salt, ginger and cloves. Mix in raisins. Pour batter into pan. Bake until light brown, 25 to 30 minutes. Cool; frost with Cream Cheese Frosting. Sprinkle with nuts. Cut into bars, about 2 × 1 1/2 inches. Refrigerate any remaining bars.

CREAM CHEESE FROSTING

1 package (3 ounces) cream cheese,
    softened
1/4 cup plus 2 tablespoons margarine or
    butter, softened
1 teaspoon vanilla
2 cups powdered sugar

Mix cream cheese, margarine and vanilla. Gradually beat in powdered sugar until smooth and of spreading consistency.

Cinnamon Strips

1 cup sugar
1 cup margarine or butter, softened
1 egg, separated
2 cups all-purpose flour
1/2 teaspoon ground cinnamon
1 tablespoon water
1/2 cup very finely chopped walnuts

Heat oven to 350°. Mix sugar, margarine and egg yolk. Stir in flour and cinnamon. Press in lightly greased jelly roll pan, 15 1/2 × 10 1/2 × 1 inch. (Or use 2 baking pans, one 8 × 8 × 2 inches and one 9 × 9 × 2 inches.) Beat egg white and water until foamy; brush over dough. Sprinkle with walnuts. Bake until very light brown, 20 to 25 minutes. Immediately cut into strips, 3 × 1 inch.

Following pages: Cinnamon Strips (right) and Date-Nut Pinwheels (left)

Banana–Sour Cream Bars

72 BARS

1 1/2 cups sugar
1 cup dairy sour cream
1/2 cup margarine or butter, softened
2 eggs
1 1/2 cups mashed bananas (about 3 large)
2 teaspoons vanilla
2 cups all-purpose flour
1 teaspoon salt
1 teaspoon baking soda
1/2 cup chopped nuts
Vanilla Frosting (below)

Heat oven to 375°. Mix sugar, sour cream, margarine and eggs in large mixer bowl on low speed, scraping bowl occasionally, 1 minute. Beat in bananas and vanilla on low speed 30 seconds. Beat in flour, salt and baking soda on medium speed, scraping bowl occasionally, 1 minute. Stir in nuts. Spread in greased and floured jelly roll pan, 15 1/2 × 10 1/2 × 1 inch. Bake until light brown, 20 to 25 minutes; cool. Frost with Vanilla Frosting. Cut into bars, 2 × 1 inch.

VANILLA FROSTING

2 cups powdered sugar
1/4 cup margarine or butter, softened
1 1/2 teaspoons vanilla
2 tablespoons hot water

Mix powdered sugar, margarine, vanilla and hot water. Stir in 1 to 2 teaspoons additional hot water until smooth and of desired consistency.

Spicy Raisin Bars

36 BARS

2 cups raisins
1 1/4 cups water
1 cup packed brown sugar
1/3 cup shortening
2 cups all-purpose flour
2 teaspoons ground cinnamon
1 teaspoon salt
1 teaspoon baking soda
1 teaspoon baking powder
1/2 teaspoon ground nutmeg
1/2 teaspoon ground cloves
1/2 cup chopped nuts, if desired
Powdered sugar

Heat oven to 350°. Mix raisins, water, brown sugar and shortening in saucepan. Heat to boiling, stirring constantly; remove from heat and cool.

Mix flour, cinnamon, salt, baking soda, baking powder, nutmeg and cloves; stir into raisin mixture. Mix in nuts. Spread in greased baking pan, 13 × 9 × 2 inches. Bake until top springs back when touched, 35 to 40 minutes; cool. Sprinkle with powdered sugar. Cut into bars, 3 × 1 inch. Store in airtight container.

Lemon Squares

1 cup all-purpose or whole wheat flour
1/2 cup margarine or butter, softened
1/4 cup powdered sugar
1 cup granulated sugar
2 eggs
2 teaspoons grated lemon peel, if desired
2 tablespoons lemon juice
1/2 teaspoon baking powder
1/4 teaspoon salt

Heat oven to 350°. Mix flour, margarine and powdered sugar. Press in ungreased baking pan, 8 × 8 × 2 inches, building up 1/2-inch edges. Bake 20 minutes.

Beat remaining ingredients until light and fluffy, about 3 minutes; pour over baked layer. Bake until no indentation remains when touched in center, about 25 minutes; cool. Cut into 1-inch squares.

Frosted Fruit Bars

1 cup sugar
1/3 cup shortening
1/3 cup margarine or butter, softened
1 egg
1 tablespoon grated orange peel, if
  desired
1/4 cup orange or pineapple juice
2 1/2 cups all-purpose flour
1 teaspoon baking soda
1/2 teaspoon salt
1/2 teaspoon ground cinnamon
1/2 teaspoon ground nutmeg
1 cup raisins
1 cup mixed candied fruit
Powdered Sugar Glaze (below)

Heat oven to 400°. Mix sugar, shortening, margarine, egg, orange peel and orange juice. Stir in remaining ingredients except Powdered Sugar Glaze. Spread in greased jelly roll pan, 15 1/2 × 10 1/2 × 1 inch. Bake until top springs back when touched, about 15 minutes; cool slightly. Spread with Powdered Sugar Glaze. Cut into bars, 3 × 2 inches.

POWDERED SUGAR GLAZE

1 1/2 cups powdered sugar
1/4 teaspoon vanilla
2 to 3 tablespoons milk

Beat powdered sugar, vanilla and milk until smooth and of desired consistency.

Granola-Plum Bars

48 BARS

1 cup packed brown sugar
1/2 cup margarine or butter, softened
1/4 cup shortening
2 cups granola
1 3/4 cups all-purpose flour
1 teaspoon salt
1 jar (12 ounces) plum preserves

Heat oven to 400°. Mix brown sugar, margarine and shortening. Stir in granola, flour and salt. Press half of the granola mixture in greased baking pan, 13 × 9 × 2 inches. Spread with preserves; top with remaining granola mixture, pressing lightly. Bake until light brown, 25 to 30 minutes. Cut into bars, 2 × 1 inch, while warm.

Grasshopper Bars

16 SQUARES

Deluxe Brownies (page 68)
3 cups powdered sugar
1/3 cup margarine or butter, softened
2 tablespoons green crème de menthe
2 tablespoons white crème de cacao
1 1/2 ounces unsweetened
* chocolate*

Prepare Deluxe Brownies as directed; cool. Mix remaining ingredients except chocolate; spread over brownies. Refrigerate 15 minutes.

Heat chocolate over low heat until melted; spread evenly over powdered sugar mixture. Refrigerate at least 3 hours. Cut into about 2-inch squares.

Chocolate Chip Bars

36 BARS

1/2 cup granulated sugar
1/3 cup packed brown sugar
1/2 cup margarine or butter, softened
1 teaspoon vanilla
1 egg
1 1/4 cups all-purpose flour
1/2 teaspoon baking soda
1/2 teaspoon salt
1/2 cup chopped nuts
1 package (6 ounces) semisweet chocolate
* chips*

Heat oven to 375°. Grease and flour baking pan, 13 × 9 × 2 inches. Mix sugars, margarine and vanilla. Beat in egg. Stir in flour, baking soda and salt. Mix in nuts and chocolate chips. Spread dough in pan. Bake until light brown, 12 to 14 minutes. Cool; cut into bars, about 2 × 1 1/2 inches.

· 2 ·

ROLLED COOKIES

Sugar Cookies

1½ cups powdered sugar
1 cup margarine or butter, softened
1 egg
1 teaspoon vanilla
½ teaspoon almond extract
2½ cups all-purpose or whole wheat
   flour
1 teaspoon baking soda
1 teaspoon cream of tartar
Granulated sugar

Mix powdered sugar, margarine, egg, vanilla and almond extract. Stir in flour, baking soda and cream of tartar. Cover and refrigerate at least 3 hours.

Heat oven to 375°. Divide dough into halves. Roll each half ³⁄₁₆ inch thick on lightly floured, cloth-covered board. Cut into desired shapes with 2- to 2½-inch cookie cutters; sprinkle with granulated sugar. Place on lightly greased cookie sheet. Bake until edges are light brown, 7 to 8 minutes.

DECORATED SUGAR COOKIES: Omit granulated sugar. Frost and decorate cooled cookies with Creamy Vanilla Frosting (below) tinted with food color, if desired. Decorate with colored sugar, small candies, candied fruit or nuts, if desired.

CREAMY VANILLA FROSTING

3 cups powdered sugar
⅓ cup margarine or butter, softened
1½ teaspoons vanilla
About 2 tablespoons milk

Mix powdered sugar and margarine. Stir in vanilla and milk; beat until smooth and of spreading consistency.

Light Ginger Cookies

1 cup powdered sugar
1 cup margarine or butter, softened
1 tablespoon vinegar
2 1/4 cups all-purpose flour
1 1/2 to 2 teaspoons ground ginger
3/4 teaspoon baking soda
1/4 teaspoon salt
Decorators' Frosting (page 28)

Heat oven to 400°. Mix powdered sugar, margarine and vinegar. Stir in remaining ingredients except Decorators' Frosting. (If dough is too dry, work in milk or cream, 1 teaspoon at a time.) Roll 1/8 inch thick on lightly floured, cloth-covered board. Cut into desired shapes with cookie cutters. Place on ungreased cookie sheet. Bake until light brown, 6 to 8 minutes. Cool slightly; carefully remove from cookie sheet. Decorate with Decorators' Frosting, if desired.

Crisp Ginger Cookies

1/3 cup molasses
1/4 cup shortening
2 tablespoons packed brown sugar
1 1/4 cups all-purpose or whole wheat
    flour
1/2 teaspoon salt
1/4 teaspoon baking soda
1/4 teaspoon baking powder
1/4 teaspoon ground cinnamon
1/4 teaspoon ground ginger
1/4 teaspoon ground cloves
Dash of ground nutmeg
Dash of ground allspice
Easy Creamy Frosting (below)

Mix molasses, shortening and brown sugar. Stir in remaining ingredients except Easy Creamy Frosting. Cover and refrigerate at least 4 hours.

Heat oven to 375°. Roll dough 1/8 inch thick or paper-thin on floured, cloth-covered board. Cut into 3-inch rounds with floured cutter. Place about 1/2 inch apart on ungreased cookie sheet. Bake until light brown, 1/8-inch-thick cookies about 8 minutes, paper-thin cookies about 5 minutes. Remove immediately from cookie sheet; cool. Frost with Easy Creamy Frosting.

EASY CREAMY FROSTING

1 cup powdered sugar
1/2 teaspoon vanilla
1/4 teaspoon salt
1 to 2 tablespoons half-and-half

Mix powdered sugar, vanilla and salt. Beat in half-and-half until smooth and of spreading consistency.

Gingerbread Boys and Girls

ABOUT 2½ DOZEN COOKIES

1½ cups dark molasses
1 cup packed brown sugar
⅔ cup cold water
⅓ cup shortening
7 cups all-purpose flour
2 teaspoons baking soda
2 teaspoons ground ginger
1 teaspoon salt
1 teaspoon ground allspice
1 teaspoon ground cloves
1 teaspoon ground cinnamon
Easy Frosting (below)

Mix molasses, brown sugar, water and shortening. Stir in remaining ingredients except Easy Frosting. Cover and refrigerate at least 2 hours.

Heat oven to 350°. Roll dough ¼ inch thick on floured board. Cut with floured gingerbread cookie cutter or other favorite cutter. Place about 2 inches apart on lightly greased cookie sheet. Bake until no indentation remains when touched, 10 to 12 minutes; cool. Frost with Easy Frosting.

EASY FROSTING

4 cups powdered sugar
1 teaspoon vanilla
5 to 6 tablespoons half-and-half

Beat powdered sugar, vanilla and half-and-half until smooth and of spreading consistency. Tint with food color if desired.

Snowflake Molasses Cookies

ABOUT 5 DOZEN 3-INCH COOKIES

⅔ cup packed brown sugar
⅔ cup shortening
1⅓ cups molasses
2 eggs
5½ cups all-purpose flour
4 teaspoons ground cinnamon
2 teaspoons ground ginger
2 teaspoons baking soda
1 teaspoon salt
Baked-on Decorators' Frosting (page 25)

Mix brown sugar, shortening and molasses. Stir in remaining ingredients except Decorators' Frosting. Cover and refrigerate at least 1 hour.

Heat oven to 375°. Roll dough ¼ inch thick on lightly floured, cloth-covered board. Cut into desired shapes with cookie cutters. Place frosting in decorators' tube with #3 writing tip. Make designs on unbaked rolled cookies. Place about 1 inch apart on lightly greased cookie sheet. Bake until no indentation remains when touched, 7 to 8 minutes; cool.

Note: For crisper cookies, roll dough ⅛ inch thick; bake 6 to 7 minutes.

BAKED-ON DECORATORS' FROSTING

⅔ cup all-purpose flour
⅔ cup margarine or butter, softened
1 tablespoon hot water
4 to 6 drops food color

Mix flour and margarine until smooth. Stir in hot water and, if desired, food color.

Frosted Molasses Cookies

ABOUT 6 DOZEN COOKIES

1½ cups sugar
1 cup shortening
2 eggs
½ cup molasses
3 teaspoons baking soda
½ cup water
5½ cups all-purpose flour
1½ teaspoons ground cinnamon
1 teaspoon ground ginger
1 teaspoon ground cloves
1 teaspoon salt
Frosting (below)

Mix sugar, shortening, eggs and molasses. Dissolve baking soda in water; stir into molasses mixture. Stir in remaining ingredients except Frosting. Cover and refrigerate at least 2 hours.

Heat oven to 375°. Roll dough ¼ inch thick on lightly floured, cloth-covered board. Cut with floured 2¾-inch round cookie cutter or other favorite cutter. Place about 2 inches apart on lightly greased cookie sheet. Bake until light brown, 8 to 10 minutes. Cool; generously frost bottoms of cookies with Frosting. Let stand 2 to 3 hours before storing to allow frosting to dry.

FROSTING

1 envelope plus 2 teaspoons unflavored gelatin
1 cup cold water
1 cup granulated sugar
2¼ cups powdered sugar
1½ teaspoons vanilla
1 teaspoon baking powder
⅛ teaspoon salt

Sprinkle gelatin on cold water in 2-quart saucepan to soften; stir in granulated sugar. Heat to rolling boil; reduce heat. Simmer uncovered 10 minutes. Pour hot mixture over powdered sugar in large bowl; beat until foamy, about 2 minutes. Beat in remaining ingredients on high speed until soft peaks form, 12 to 15 minutes.

Following pages: Frosted Molasses Cookies, Gingerbread Boys and Girls and Snowflake Molasses Cookies

Sour Cream Cookies

1 cup sugar
¼ cup margarine or butter, softened
¼ cup shortening
1 egg
1 teaspoon vanilla
2⅔ cups all-purpose flour
1 teaspoon baking powder
½ teaspoon baking soda
½ teaspoon salt
¼ teaspoon ground nutmeg
½ cup dairy sour cream
Decorators' Frosting (below)

DECORATORS' FROSTING

2 cups powdered sugar
2 to 3 tablespoons water

Heat oven to 425°. Mix 1 cup sugar, the margarine, shortening, egg and vanilla. Stir in remaining ingredients except frosting. Divide dough into 3 equal parts. Roll each part ¼ inch thick on lightly floured, cloth-covered board. Cut into desired shapes with 2-inch cookie cutter; pipe with Decorators' Frosting. Place about 1 inch apart on ungreased cookie sheet. Bake until no indentation remains when touched, 6 to 8 minutes.

Mix powdered sugar and water until frosting is of a consistency that can be used easily in a decorators' tube or envelope cone and yet hold its shape. To make an envelope cone, place about ⅓ cup frosting in the corner of an envelope; fold sides toward center. Snip off corner to make tip.

CHOCOLATE–SOUR CREAM COOKIES: Mix 1 ounce melted unsweetened chocolate (cool) into 1 part dough.

COCONUT–SOUR CREAM COOKIES: Mix ¼ cup flaked coconut into 1 part dough.

HANDPRINT COOKIES: Use the basic dough or any of the flavored variations. After rolling, trace around hand with knife or pastry wheel. Cut remaining dough into desired shapes. Makes about 6 Handprint Cookies and 1 dozen 2-inch cookies.

Cream Wafers

2 cups all-purpose flour
1 cup margarine or butter, softened
1/3 cup whipping cream
Sugar
Filling (below)

Mix flour, margarine and cream. Cover and refrigerate.

Heat oven to 375°. Roll about 1/3 of the dough at a time 1/8 inch thick on floured, cloth-covered board (keep remaining dough refrigerated). Cut into 1 1/2-inch rounds. Coat both sides with sugar. Place on ungreased cookie sheet. Prick each round with fork about 4 times. Bake just until set but not brown, 7 to 9 minutes. Remove from cookie sheet; cool. Put cookies together in pairs with Filling.

FILLING

3/4 cup powdered sugar
1/4 cup margarine or butter, softened
1 teaspoon vanilla
Few drops water, if desired
Food color

Mix powdered sugar, margarine and vanilla until smooth and fluffy. Beat in water, if necessary, until smooth and of spreading consistency. Tint parts of filling with few drops different food colors.

Scotch Shortbread

3/4 cup margarine or butter, softened
1/4 cup sugar
2 cups all-purpose flour

Heat oven to 350°. Mix margarine and sugar. Work in flour with hands. (If dough is crumbly, mix in 1 to 2 tablespoons margarine or butter, softened.) Roll 1/2 to 1/3 inch thick on lightly floured, cloth-covered board. Cut into small shapes (leaves, ovals, squares, triangles, etc.). Place 1/2 inch apart on ungreased cookie sheet. Bake until set, about 20 minutes. Remove immediately from cookie sheet.

Raspberry-Orange Turnovers

½ cup margarine or butter, softened
1 package (3 ounces) cream cheese,
  softened
1 teaspoon finely grated orange peel
1 cup all-purpose flour
⅛ teaspoon salt
¼ cup raspberry preserves
Orange Glaze (below)

Mix margarine, cream cheese, orange peel, flour and salt. Cover and refrigerate at least 1 hour.

Heat oven to 375°. Roll dough ⅛ inch thick on lightly floured, cloth-covered board; cut into 2½-inch circles. Spoon about ½ teaspoon preserves onto each circle; moisten edge on half of each circle and fold dough over preserves. Press edges together. Place 1 inch apart on ungreased baking sheet. Bake until edges are light brown, 8 to 10 minutes. Remove immediately from baking sheet; cool. Drizzle cookies with Orange Glaze.

ORANGE GLAZE

1 cup powdered sugar
1 teaspoon finely grated orange peel
2 tablespoons orange juice

Mix powdered sugar, grated orange peel and orange juice until smooth and of desired consistency.

Bear Claws

½ cup granulated sugar
¼ cup margarine or butter, softened
2 tablespoons shortening
1 egg
1 teaspoon vanilla
1¼ cups all-purpose flour
½ teaspoon baking powder
½ teaspoon salt
About 3 tablespoons raspberry jam
About 3 tablespoons chopped nuts
About 3 tablespoons powdered sugar

Mix granulated sugar, margarine, shortening, egg and vanilla. Stir in flour, baking powder and salt. Cover and refrigerate at least 1 hour.

Heat oven to 400°. Roll dough into 12-inch square on lightly floured, cloth-covered board. Cut into 3-inch squares. Spread about ½ teaspoon jam down center of each square; sprinkle with about ½ teaspoon nuts. Fold 1 edge of dough over filling; fold other edge over top. Place on greased cookie sheet. Make 4 or 5 cuts in 1 long side of each cookie; spread cuts slightly apart. Sprinkle each cookie with about ½ teaspoon powdered sugar. Bake until light brown, about 6 minutes.

PINWHEELS: Cut unfolded 3-inch squares diagonally from each corner almost to center. Fold every other point to center to make pinwheel. Spoon ½ teaspoon jam onto center of each pinwheel; sprinkle with ½ teaspoon nuts and ½ teaspoon powdered sugar. Bake as directed.

LOLLIPOPS: Drop dough by teaspoonfuls onto ungreased cookie sheet; flatten slightly. Place 1 wooden ice-cream stick and 1 milk chocolate star on each circle. Top with another teaspoonful dough; press together. Bake until light brown, about 8 minutes.

MEXICAN COOKIES: Substitute anise extract for the vanilla. Cut 12-inch square into 3-inch flower shapes with cookie cutter; sprinkle with colored sugar. Bake as directed.

Following pages: Bear Claws (right) *and Raspberry-Orange Turnovers* (left)

Hamantaschen

1 cup sugar
⅓ cup vegetable oil
3 eggs
Grated peel and juice from 1 orange
3 ¼ cups all-purpose flour
2 teaspoons baking powder
½ teaspoon salt
Filling (below)

Beat sugar, oil and eggs until blended. Stir in orange peel and orange juice. Mix in flour, baking powder and salt. Cover and refrigerate at least 2 hours.

Heat oven to 375°. Divide dough into halves. Roll each half ⅛ inch thick on lightly floured, cloth-covered board. Cut into 3-inch rounds. Spoon 1 teaspoon Filling onto each round. Fold each round to form triangle. Pinch edges together to form slight ridge. Place on lightly greased cookie sheet. Bake until golden brown, 12 to 15 minutes.

FILLING

1 pound cut-up cooked prunes
1 cup chopped nuts
1 tablespoon sugar
1 tablespoon lemon juice

Mix all ingredients.

· 3 ·

DROP COOKIES

Chocolate Chip Cookies

ABOUT 6 DOZEN COOKIES

1 cup margarine or butter, softened
³/₄ cup granulated sugar
³/₄ cup packed brown sugar
1 egg
2 ¹/₄ cups all-purpose flour
1 teaspoon baking soda
¹/₂ teaspoon salt
1 cup coarsely chopped nuts
1 package (12 ounces) semisweet chocolate chips

Heat oven to 375°. Mix margarine, sugars and egg. Stir in flour, baking soda and salt (dough will be stiff). Stir in nuts and chocolate chips. Drop dough by rounded teaspoonfuls about 2 inches apart onto ungreased cookie sheet. Bake until light brown, 8 to 10 minutes. (Centers will be soft.) Cool slightly; remove from cookie sheet.

Candy Cookies

ABOUT 3 DOZEN COOKIES

¹/₂ cup granulated sugar
¹/₂ cup packed brown sugar
¹/₃ cup margarine or butter, softened
¹/₃ cup shortening
1 teaspoon vanilla
1 egg
1 ¹/₂ cups all-purpose flour
¹/₂ teaspoon baking soda
¹/₂ teaspoon salt
1 package (8 ounces) chocolate-coated candies

Heat oven to 375°. Mix sugars, margarine, shortening, vanilla and egg. Stir in remaining ingredients. Drop dough by heaping teaspoonfuls about 2 inches apart onto ungreased cookie sheet. Bake until light brown, 8 to 10 minutes. (Centers will be soft.) Cool slightly; remove from cookie sheet.

Oatmeal Cookies

½ cup granulated sugar
½ cup packed brown sugar
¼ cup margarine or butter, softened
¼ cup shortening
½ teaspoon baking soda
½ teaspoon ground cinnamon
½ teaspoon vanilla
¼ teaspoon baking powder
¼ teaspoon salt
1 egg
1½ cups quick-cooking oats
1 cup all-purpose flour
1 cup raisins or chopped nuts

Heat oven to 375°. Mix all ingredients except oats, flour and raisins. Stir in oats, flour and, if desired, raisins. Drop dough by rounded teaspoonfuls about 2 inches apart onto ungreased cookie sheet. Bake until light brown, about 10 minutes. Remove immediately from cookie sheet.

OATMEAL CRISPIES: Omit cinnamon and raisins.

OATMEAL SQUARES: Press dough in ungreased square pan, 8 × 8 × 2 inches. Bake until light brown, about 25 minutes. Cut into about 2-inch squares while warm. Makes 16 squares.

Hermits

1 cup packed brown sugar
¼ cup margarine or butter, softened
¼ cup shortening
¼ cup cold coffee
1 egg
½ teaspoon ground cinnamon
½ teaspoon ground nutmeg
1¾ cups all-purpose flour
½ teaspoon baking soda
½ teaspoon salt
1¼ cups raisins
¾ cup chopped nuts

Heat oven to 375°. Mix brown sugar, margarine, shortening, coffee, egg, cinnamon and nutmeg. Stir in remaining ingredients. Drop dough by rounded teaspoonfuls about 2 inches apart onto ungreased cookie sheet. Bake until almost no indentation remains when touched, 8 to 10 minutes. Remove immediately from cookie sheet.

Fruit-filled Drops

*Date Filling or Pineapple-Cherry Filling
(below)*
2 cups packed brown sugar
1 cup shortening
2 eggs
½ cup water or buttermilk
1 teaspoon vanilla
3½ cups all-purpose flour
1 teaspoon salt
1 teaspoon baking soda
⅛ teaspoon ground cinnamon

Prepare Date Filling; cool. Heat oven to 400°. Mix brown sugar, shortening and eggs. Stir in water and vanilla. Mix in remaining ingredients. Drop by teaspoonfuls about 2 inches apart onto ungreased cookie sheet. Top each teaspoonful of dough with ½ teaspoon filling. Top filling with ½ teaspoon dough. Bake 10 to 12 minutes. Remove immediately from cookie sheet.

DATE FILLING

2 cups snipped dates
¾ cup sugar
¾ cup water
½ cup chopped nuts

Cook dates, sugar and water over low heat, stirring constantly, until thickened. Stir in nuts.

PINEAPPLE-CHERRY FILLING

*1 can (8¼ ounces) crushed pineapple
(with syrup)*
*¼ cup cut-up candied cherries or
chopped maraschino cherries*
½ cup sugar
½ cup chopped nuts

Cook pineapple, cherries and sugar in saucepan over low heat, stirring constantly, until thickened. Stir in nuts.

Applesauce-Spice Drops

2 cups packed brown sugar
1 cup shortening
½ cup cold coffee
2 cups applesauce
2 eggs
3½ cups all-purpose flour
1 teaspoon baking soda
1 teaspoon salt
1 teaspoon ground cinnamon
1 teaspoon ground nutmeg
1 teaspoon ground cloves
1 cup raisins
½ cup coarsely chopped nuts

Heat oven to 400°. Mix brown sugar, shortening, coffee, applesauce and eggs. Stir in remaining ingredients (dough will be very soft). Drop by rounded teaspoonfuls about 2 inches apart onto lightly greased cookie sheet. Bake until almost no indentation remains when touched, about 7 minutes.

Glazed Cranberry Cookies

1 cup granulated sugar
¾ cup packed brown sugar
½ cup margarine or butter, softened
¼ cup milk
2 tablespoons orange juice
1 egg
3 cups all-purpose flour
1 teaspoon baking powder
½ teaspoon salt
¼ teaspoon baking soda
2½ cups coarsely chopped cranberries
1 cup chopped nuts
Browned Butter Glaze (page 39)

Heat oven to 375°. Mix sugars and margarine. Stir in milk, orange juice and egg. Stir in remaining ingredients except Browned Butter Glaze. Drop by rounded teaspoonfuls about 2 inches apart onto greased cookie sheet. Bake until light brown, 10 to 15 minutes. Cool; spread with glaze, if desired.

BROWNED BUTTER GLAZE

1/3 cup margarine or butter
2 cups powdered sugar
1 1/2 teaspoons vanilla
2 to 4 tablespoons hot water

Heat margarine over low heat until golden brown; cool slightly. Stir in powdered sugar and vanilla. Beat in hot water until smooth and of desired consistency.

Sesame Seed Drops

ABOUT 3 DOZEN COOKIES

1/2 cup margarine or butter
1/3 cup sesame seed
1/2 cup margarine or butter, softened
1 cup sugar
1 egg
2 tablespoons water
2 cups all-purpose flour
1 teaspoon baking powder
1/4 teaspoon salt
Sesame Frosting (below)

Heat oven to 375°. Heat 1/2 cup margarine and the sesame seed over low heat, stirring occasionally, until margarine is golden brown (watch carefully to avoid burning); remove from heat. Remove 2 tablespoons sesame seed, draining margarine. Reserve remaining sesame seed mixture.

Mix the 2 tablespoons sesame seed, 1/2 cup softened margarine, the sugar, egg and water. Stir in flour, baking powder and salt. Drop by rounded teaspoonfuls about 2 inches apart onto ungreased cookie sheet; flatten each with greased bottom of glass dipped in sugar. Bake until edges are light brown, about 10 minutes; cool. Frost with Sesame Frosting.

SESAME FROSTING

3 cups powdered sugar
3 tablespoons milk
1 teaspoon vanilla
Reserved sesame seed mixture

Beat powdered sugar, milk, vanilla and sesame seed mixture until frosting is of spreading consistency.

Following pages: Sesame Seed Drops

Coconut Macaroons

3 ½ TO 4 DOZEN COOKIES

3 egg whites
1/4 teaspoon cream of tartar
1/8 teaspoon salt
3/4 cup sugar
1/4 teaspoon almond extract
3 drops red or green food color
2 cups flaked coconut
12 candied cherries, each cut into
    fourths

Beat egg whites, cream of tartar and salt in 1 ½-quart bowl until foamy. Beat in sugar, 1 tablespoon at a time; continue beating until stiff and glossy. Do not underbeat. Pour into 2½-quart bowl. Fold in almond extract, food color (if desired) and coconut.

Heat oven to 300°. Drop mixture by teaspoonfuls about 1 inch apart onto aluminum foil-covered cookie sheet. Place a cherry piece on each cookie. Bake just until edges are light brown, 20 to 25 minutes. Cool 10 minutes; remove from foil.

Note: Store cookies in airtight container no longer than 2 weeks or freeze no longer than 1 month.

Sour Cream Drops

4 ½ TO 5 DOZEN COOKIES

2 3/4 cups all-purpose flour
1 1/2 cups packed brown sugar
1 cup dairy sour cream
1/2 cup shortening
1 teaspoon salt
1 teaspoon vanilla
1/2 teaspoon baking soda
2 eggs
1 cup chopped nuts, if desired
Maple Butter Glaze (below)

Mix all ingredients except Maple Butter Glaze. (If dough is soft, cover and refrigerate.) Heat oven to 375°. Drop by level tablespoonfuls about 2 inches apart onto ungreased cookie sheet. Bake until amost no indentation remains when touched, about 10 minutes. Remove immediately from cookie sheet; cool. Spread with Maple Butter Glaze.

MAPLE BUTTER GLAZE

1/2 cup butter
2 cups powdered sugar
2 teaspoons maple flavoring
2 to 4 tablespoons hot water

Heat butter over low heat until golden brown; remove from heat. Stir in powdered sugar and maple flavoring. Beat in hot water until smooth and of desired consistency.

MAPLE DROPS: Substitute 1 tablespoon maple flavoring for the vanilla.

PEANUT DROPS: Substitute salted peanuts for the nuts.

RAISIN–SOUR CREAM DROPS: Mix in 1 cup raisins.

SPICY SUGAR DROPS: Mix ½ cup sugar, 1 teaspoon ground cinnamon and ¼ teaspoon ground cloves; sprinkle over cookies before baking. Omit glaze.

APPLESAUCE DROPS: Omit sour cream. Mix in ¾ cup applesauce, 1 teaspoon ground cinnamon, ¼ teaspoon ground cloves and 1 cup raisins.

Ginger Creams

½ cup sugar
½ cup molasses
½ cup water
⅓ cup shortening
1 egg
2 cups all-purpose or whole wheat flour
1 teaspoon ground ginger
½ teaspoon salt
½ teaspoon baking soda
½ teaspoon ground nutmeg
½ teaspoon ground cloves
½ teaspoon ground cinnamon
Creamy Vanilla Frosting (page 22)

Mix sugar, molasses, water, shortening and egg. Stir in remaining ingredients except Creamy Vanilla Frosting. Cover and refrigerate at least 1 hour.

Heat oven to 400°. Drop by teaspoonfuls about 2 inches apart onto ungreased cookie sheet. Bake until almost no indentation remains when touched, about 8 minutes. Remove immediately from cookie sheet; cool. Frost with Creamy Vanilla Frosting.

Following pages: Ginger Creams

Banana-Oatmeal Drops

ABOUT 4 DOZEN COOKIES

1 ¾ cups regular or quick-cooking oats
1 ½ cups all-purpose flour
1 cup sugar
1 cup mashed bananas (2 to 3 medium)
¾ cup shortening
1 egg
1 teaspoon salt
1 teaspoon ground cinnamon
½ teaspoon baking soda
¼ teaspoon ground nutmeg
½ cup chopped nuts or raisins

Heat oven to 400°. Mix all ingredients. Drop by rounded teaspoonfuls about 2 inches apart onto ungreased cookie sheet. Bake until light brown, about 10 minutes.

BANANA–CHOCOLATE CHIP DROPS: Substitute semisweet chocolate chips for the nuts.

BANANA-GRANOLA DROPS: Heat oven to 375°. Omit oats and nuts. Mix in 2 cups granola and 1 teaspoon vanilla. Bake until almost no indentation remains when touched, 8 to 10 minutes. Remove immediately from cookie sheet. Makes about 3 ½ dozen cookies.

Soft Pumpkin Drops

ABOUT 4 DOZEN COOKIES

1 cup sugar
1 cup canned pumpkin
½ cup shortening
1 tablespoon grated orange peel
2 cups all-purpose or whole wheat flour
1 teaspoon baking powder
1 teaspoon baking soda
1 teaspoon ground cinnamon
¼ teaspoon salt
½ cup raisins
½ cup chopped nuts
Creamy Vanilla Frosting (page 22)

Heat oven to 375°. Mix sugar, pumpkin, shortening and orange peel. Stir in flour, baking powder, baking soda, cinnamon and salt. Mix in raisins and nuts. Drop by rounded teaspoonfuls about 2 inches apart onto ungreased cookie sheet. Bake until light brown, 8 to 10 minutes; cool. Frost with Creamy Vanilla Frosting.

CHOCOLATE CHIP–PUMPKIN DROPS: Substitute semisweet chocolate chips for the raisins or nuts.

· 4 ·

CHOCOLATE COOKIES

Chocolate Crinkles

ABOUT 6 DOZEN COOKIES

2 cups granulated sugar
1/2 cup vegetable oil
4 ounces unsweetened chocolate, melted
   and cooled
2 teaspoons vanilla
4 eggs
2 cups all-purpose flour
2 teaspoons baking powder
1/2 teaspoon salt
1 cup powdered sugar

Mix granulated sugar, oil, chocolate and vanilla. Mix in eggs, 1 at a time. Stir in flour, baking powder and salt. Cover and refrigerate at least 3 hours.

Heat oven to 350°. Drop dough by teaspoonfuls into powdered sugar; roll around to coat. Shape into balls. Place about 2 inches apart on greased cookie sheet. Bake until almost no indentation remains when touched, 10 to 12 minutes.

Two-Way Chocolate Cookies

ABOUT 3 TO 4 DOZEN COOKIES

1 cup sugar
1/2 cup margarine or butter, softened
1/3 cup milk
4 ounces unsweetened chocolate, melted
   and cooled
1 egg
1 teaspoon vanilla
2 cups all-purpose flour
1/2 teaspoon baking powder
1/2 teaspoon salt
1 cup chopped pecans

Mix sugar, margarine, milk, chocolate, egg and vanilla in large mixer bowl. Beat in remaining ingredients on low speed, scraping bowl constantly, until soft dough forms. Use half of the dough for Caramelitas and half for Coco-Nut Balls (below).

CARAMELITAS

1/2 chocolate dough (above)
18 vanilla caramels or candied cherries,
   cut into halves
1 1/2 cups powdered sugar
1 ounce unsweetened chocolate, melted
   and cooled
2 tablespoons light corn syrup
2 to 3 tablespoons hot water

Cover and refrigerate dough at least 1 hour. Heat oven to 400°. Shape dough by rounded teaspoonfuls around caramel halves. Place on ungreased cookie sheet. Bake until set, about 7 minutes; cool. Beat remaining ingredients in small bowl until thickened. Swirl tops of cookies in chocolate mixture.

COCO-NUT BALLS

2 cups flaked coconut
1/2 chocolate dough (above)

Heat oven to 400°. Work the coconut into the chocolate dough. Shape dough by rounded teaspoonfuls into balls. Roll balls in additional coconut if desired. Place on ungreased cookie sheet. Bake until set, about 7 minutes.

48   BETTY CROCKER'S RED SPOON COLLECTION

Chocolate Drops

1 cup sugar
½ cup margarine or butter, softened
⅓ cup buttermilk or water
1 egg
*2 ounces unsweetened chocolate, melted
and cooled*
1 teaspoon vanilla
*1¾ cups all-purpose or whole wheat
flour*
½ teaspoon baking soda
½ teaspoon salt
1 cup chopped nuts, if desired
*Chocolate Frosting or Browned Butter
Frosting (below)*

Heat oven to 400°. Mix sugar, margarine, buttermilk, egg, chocolate and vanilla. Stir in flour, baking soda, salt and nuts. Drop by rounded teaspoonfuls about 2 inches apart onto ungreased cookie sheet. Bake until almost no indentation remains when touched, 8 to 10 minutes. Remove immediately from cookie sheet; cool. Frost with Chocolate Frosting.

CHOCOLATE FROSTING

2 ounces unsweetened chocolate
2 tablespoons margarine or butter
3 tablespoons water
2 cups powdered sugar

Heat chocolate and margarine over low heat until melted; remove from heat. Beat in water and powdered sugar until smooth and of spreading consistency.

BROWNED BUTTER FROSTING

¼ cup butter
2 cups powdered sugar
1 teaspoon vanilla
2 tablespoons half-and-half

Heat butter over low heat until golden brown; remove from heat. Beat in powdered sugar, vanilla and half-and-half until smooth and of spreading consistency.

CHOCOLATE-CHERRY DROPS: Substitute 2 cups cut-up candied or maraschino cherries for the nuts. Use Chocolate Frosting.

CHOCOLATE-PEANUT DROPS: Omit salt. Substitute 2 cups salted peanuts for the nuts. Use Chocolate Frosting.

Chocolate Cookie Slices

1 1/2 cups powdered sugar
1 1/4 cups margarine or butter, softened
1 egg
3 cups all-purpose flour
1/2 cup cocoa
1/4 teaspoon salt
1 1/2 cups finely chopped pecans
Fudge Frosting (below)

Mix powdered sugar, margarine and egg. Stir in flour, cocoa and salt. Cover and refrigerate 1 hour.

Divide into halves. Shape each half into roll, about 1 1/2 inches in diameter. Roll in pecans. Wrap and refrigerate at least 8 hours but no longer than 6 weeks.

Heat oven to 400°. Cut rolls into 1/8-inch slices. (If dough crumbles while cutting, let warm slightly.) Place about 1 inch apart on ungreased cookie sheet. Bake about 8 minutes. Remove immediately from cookie sheet; cool. Frost with Fudge Frosting, if desired.

FUDGE FROSTING

1 cup sugar
1/3 cup milk
1/4 cup shortening
2 ounces unsweetened chocolate
1/4 teaspoon salt
1 teaspoon vanilla

Heat sugar, milk, shortening, chocolate and salt to rolling boil, stirring occasionally. Boil 1 minute without stirring. Place pan in bowl of ice and water. Beat until thick and cold; stir in vanilla.

TWO-TONE PINWHEELS: Omit 1/2 cup cocoa and the pecans. After dough is mixed, divide into halves. Stir 1/4 cup cocoa into 1 half. Cover and refrigerate 1 hour. Roll plain dough into rectangle, about 16 × 9 inches, on lightly floured board. Repeat with chocolate dough; place on plain dough. Roll doughs together to 3/16-inch thickness. Roll up tightly, beginning at long side. Wrap and refrigerate. Continue as directed. Omit frosting.

Chocolate-Mint Cookies

ABOUT 3 DOZEN COOKIES

1 cup sugar
1/2 cup margarine or butter, softened
1 teaspoon vanilla
1 egg
2 ounces unsweetened chocolate,
    melted and cooled
1 cup all-purpose flour
1/2 teaspoon salt
Peppermint Frosting (below)
1/4 cup margarine or butter
2 tablespoons corn syrup
1 package (6 ounces) semisweet chocolate
    chips

PEPPERMINT FROSTING

2 1/2 cups powdered sugar
1/4 cup margarine or butter, softened
3 tablespoons milk
1/2 teaspoon peppermint extract

Heat oven to 375°. Mix sugar, 1/2 cup margarine, the vanilla, egg and unsweetened chocolate. Stir in flour and salt. Drop dough by rounded teaspoonfuls about 2 inches apart onto ungreased cookie sheet. Flatten each cookie with greased bottom of glass dipped in sugar. Bake until set, about 8 minutes. Cool slightly; remove from cookie sheet. Cool cookies completely.

Spread Peppermint Frosting over each cookie to within 1/4 inch of edge. Heat 1/4 cup margarine, the corn syrup and chocolate chips over low heat, stirring constantly, until margarine and chocolate are melted. Drizzle over cookies.

Mix all ingredients until smooth and of spreading consistency.

Chocolate-Peppermint Pretzels

ABOUT 4 DOZEN COOKIES

1 cup powdered sugar
1/2 cup margarine or butter, softened
1/2 cup shortening
1 egg
1 1/2 teaspoons vanilla
2 1/2 cups all-purpose flour
1/2 cup cocoa
1 teaspoon salt
Chocolate Frosting (page 49)
1/4 cup crushed peppermint candy

Mix powdered sugar, margarine, shortening, egg and vanilla. Stir in flour, cocoa and salt. Knead level tablespoonful of dough with hands until right consistency for molding. Roll into pencil-like rope, about 9 inches long, on board. Twist into pretzel shape on ungreased cookie sheet. Repeat with remaining dough.

Heat oven to 375°. Bake until set, about 9 minutes. Let stand 1 to 2 minutes before removing from cookie sheet; cool. Prepare Chocolate Frosting and thin with 1 tablespoon water, if necessary. Dip tops of pretzels into Chocolate Frosting. Sprinkle with peppermint candy.

*Following pages: Chocolate Cookie Slices (**right**) and Chocolate Crinkles (**left**)*

Fudgy Oatmeal Bars

2 cups packed brown sugar
1 cup margarine or butter, softened
1 teaspoon vanilla
2 eggs
2 1/2 cups all-purpose flour
1 teaspoon baking soda
1/2 teaspoon salt
3 cups quick-cooking or regular oats
2 tablespoons margarine or butter
1 can (14 ounces) sweetened condensed
    milk
1 package (12 ounces) semisweet
    chocolate chips
1 cup chopped nuts
1 teaspoon vanilla
1/2 teaspoon salt

Heat oven to 350°. Mix brown sugar, 1 cup margarine, 1 teaspoon vanilla and the eggs. Stir in flour, baking soda and 1/2 teaspoon salt; stir in oats. Reserve 1/3 of the oat mixture. Press remaining oat mixture in greased jelly roll pan, 15 1/2 × 10 1/2 × 1 inch.

Heat 2 tablespoons margarine, the milk and chocolate chips over low heat, stirring constantly, until chocolate is melted; remove from heat. Stir in nuts, 1 teaspoon vanilla and 1/2 teaspoon salt. Spread over oat mixture in pan. Drop reserved oat mixture by rounded teaspoonfuls onto chocolate mixture.

Bake until golden brown, 25 to 30 minutes. Cut into bars, about 2 × 1 inch, while warm.

Double Chocolate Oatmeal Cookies

1 1/2 cups sugar
1 cup margarine or butter, softened
1 egg
1/4 cup water
1 teaspoon vanilla
1 1/4 cups all-purpose flour
1/3 cup cocoa
1/2 teaspoon baking soda
1/2 teaspoon salt
3 cups quick-cooking oats
1 package (6 ounces) semisweet chocolate
    chips

Heat oven to 350°. Mix sugar, margarine, egg, water and vanilla. Stir in remaining ingredients. Drop dough by rounded teaspoonfuls about 2 inches apart onto ungreased cookie sheet. Bake until almost no indentation remains when touched, 10 to 12 minutes. Remove immediately from cookie sheet.

· 5 ·

NUT COOKIES

Nut Roll-ups

3 DOZEN COOKIES

1/3 cup margarine or butter, softened
1 package (3 ounces) cream cheese,
* softened*
3/4 cup all-purpose flour
36 pecan or walnut halves, candied
* cherry halves or chocolate,*
* butterscotch-flavored or peanut*
* butter-flavored chips*
Powdered sugar

Mix margarine and cream cheese. Stir in flour until soft dough forms. Cover and refrigerate until firm, at least 8 hours.

Roll dough into rectangle, 12 × 9 inches, on cloth-covered board generously sprinkled with powdered sugar. Cut dough into rectangles, each 3 × 1 inch. Place 1 pecan half on one end of each rectangle; roll up, beginning at 1-inch end. Pinch end and sides to seal. Place cookies, end seam sides down, on ungreased cookie sheet. Bake until golden brown, 15 to 17 minutes; cool. Sprinkle with powdered sugar.

Coconut–Macadamia Nut Cookies

ABOUT 4 1/2 DOZEN COOKIES

1 cup margarine or butter, softened
1 cup packed brown sugar
1/2 cup granulated sugar
1 egg
2 1/4 cups all-purpose flour
1 teaspoon baking soda
1 cup flaked coconut
1 jar (3 1/2 ounces) macadamia nuts,
* coarsely chopped*

Heat oven to 375°. Mix margarine, sugars and egg. Stir in flour and baking soda (dough will be stiff). Stir in coconut and nuts. Drop dough by heaping teaspoonfuls about 2 inches apart onto ungreased cookie sheet. Bake until light brown, 8 to 10 minutes. (Centers will be soft.) Cool slightly; remove from cookie sheet.

Mixed Nut Squares

1 cup packed brown sugar
1 cup margarine or butter, softened
1 egg yolk
1 teaspoon vanilla
2 cups all-purpose or whole wheat flour
¼ teaspoon salt
1 package (6 ounces) butterscotch chips
½ cup light corn syrup
2 tablespoons margarine or butter
1 tablespoon water
1 can (12 ounces) salted mixed nuts

Heat oven to 350°. Mix brown sugar, 1 cup margarine, the egg yolk and vanilla. Stir in flour and salt. Press in ungreased baking pan, 13 × 9 × 2 inches. Bake until light brown, about 25 minutes; cool.

Mix butterscotch chips, corn syrup, 2 tablespoons margarine and the water in saucepan. Cook over medium heat, stirring occasionally, until butterscotch is melted; cool. Spread over baked layer. Sprinkle with nuts, pressing lightly. Refrigerate until topping is firm, about 1 hour. Cut into 2-inch squares. Store in refrigerator.

Salted Peanut Crisps

1½ cups packed brown sugar
½ cup margarine or butter, softened
½ cup shortening
2 eggs
2 teaspoons vanilla
3 cups all-purpose flour
1 teaspoon salt
½ teaspoon baking soda
2 cups salted peanuts

Heat oven to 375°. Mix brown sugar, margarine, shortening, eggs and vanilla. Stir in remaining ingredients. Drop by rounded teaspoonfuls about 2 inches apart onto lightly greased cookie sheet; flatten with greased bottom of glass dipped in sugar. Bake until golden brown, 8 to 10 minutes. Immediately remove from cookie sheet.

CHOCOLATE CHIP–PEANUT CRISPS: Stir in 1 package (6 ounces) semisweet chocolate chips.

Peanut-Honey Slices

⅔ cup peanut butter
½ cup sugar
½ cup honey or corn syrup
3 tablespoons shortening
2 tablespoons plus 1 teaspoon margarine
    or butter, softened
1 egg
2 cups all-purpose flour
1 teaspoon baking powder
½ teaspoon salt
¼ teaspoon baking soda
½ cup finely chopped peanuts

Mix peanut butter, sugar, honey, shortening, margarine and egg. Stir in remaining ingredients. Shape into strip, about 10 × 2½ × 1½ inches. Wrap and refrigerate at least 8 hours.

Heat oven to 400°. Cut strip into ⅛-inch slices. Place on ungreased cookie sheet. Bake until light brown, 6 to 7 minutes.

Rich Pecan Slices

1 cup powdered sugar
1 cup margarine or butter, softened
1 teaspoon vanilla or almond extract
2½ cups all-purpose flour
¼ teaspoon salt
1 cup finely chopped pecans

Mix powdered sugar, margarine and vanilla. Stir in flour and salt. (If dough seems dry, mix in 3 to 4 teaspoons milk.) Shape into roll, about 2 inches in diameter. Roll in pecans. Wrap and refrigerate at least 4 hours.

Heat oven to 400°. Cut roll into ⅛-inch slices. Place about 1 inch apart on ungreased cookie sheet. Bake until light brown, 8 to 10 minutes. Remove immediately from cookie sheet.

Following pages: Cashew Triangles, Caramel-Pecan Tarts and Salted Peanut Crisps

Caramel-Pecan Tarts

1 cup all-purpose flour
1/2 cup margarine or butter, softened
1/4 cup powdered sugar
3/4 cup packed brown sugar
1 tablespoon margarine or butter, softened
1 egg, slightly beaten
1 teaspoon vanilla
1/4 teaspoon salt
1/2 cup chopped pecans

Heat oven to 350°. Mix flour, 1/2 cup margarine and the powdered sugar. Divide into 24 equal pieces. Press each piece against bottom and side of ungreased small muffin cup, 1 3/4 × 1 inch. Do not allow pastry to extend above tops of cups.

Mix remaining ingredients. Spoon scant tablespoon mixture into each muffin cup. Bake until filling is set and crust is light brown, about 20 minutes. Cool in muffin cups 20 minutes. Remove from muffin cups with tip of knife; cool on wire rack.

Almond-Cherry Strips

2 1/2 cups all-purpose flour
1 cup sugar
1/2 cup whipping cream
1/4 cup margarine or butter, softened
1 egg, separated
2 teaspoons baking powder
1 teaspoon almond extract
1/2 teaspoon salt
1 3/4 cups powdered sugar
1/2 teaspoon almond extract
1/4 cup chopped almonds
1/4 cup cut-up red candied cherries

Mix flour, sugar, whipping cream, margarine, egg yolk, baking powder, 1 teaspoon almond extract and the salt. Work with hands until blended. Cover and refrigerate at least 1 hour.

Heat oven to 375°. Divide dough into halves. Roll each half into rectangle, 8 × 6 inches, on well-floured, cloth-covered board. Square off rounded corners. Place on greased cookie sheet.

Beat egg white until foamy. Beat in powdered sugar gradually; continue beating until stiff and glossy. Do not underbeat. Beat in 1/2 teaspoon almond extract. Spread egg white over dough; arrange almonds and cherries on top. Cut into strips, about 2 × 1 inch. Bake until edges are light brown, about 10 minutes.

Easy Praline Bars

48 BARS

24 graham cracker squares
1/2 cup packed brown sugar
1/2 cup margarine or butter
1/2 teaspoon vanilla
1/2 cup chopped pecans

Heat oven to 350°. Arrange crackers in single layer in ungreased jelly roll pan, 15½ × 10½ × 1 inch. Heat brown sugar and margarine to boiling. Boil and stir 1 minute; remove from heat. Stir in vanilla. Pour over crackers; spread evenly. Sprinkle with pecans. Bake until bubbly, 8 to 10 minutes; cool slightly. Cut into bars, about 2¼ × 1¼ inches.

Cashew Triangles

24 TRIANGLES

1/2 cup margarine or butter, softened
1/4 cup granulated sugar
1/4 cup packed brown sugar
1/2 teaspoon vanilla
1 egg, separated
1 cup all-purpose flour
1/8 teaspoon salt
1 teaspoon water
1 cup chopped salted cashew nuts,
    macadamia nuts or toasted almonds
1 square (1 ounce) unsweetened
    chocolate, melted

Heat oven to 350°. Mix margarine, sugars, vanilla and egg yolk. Stir in flour and salt. Press dough in ungreased rectangular pan, 13 × 9 × 2 inches, with floured hands. Beat egg white and water; brush over dough. Sprinkle with cashew nuts; press lightly. Bake until light brown, about 25 minutes; cool 10 minutes. Cut into about 3-inch squares; cut each square diagonally into halves. Remove immediately from pan; cool completely.

Drizzle with chocolate. Let stand until chocolate is set, about 2 hours.

· 6 ·

BROWNIES

Brownies

4 ounces unsweetened
  chocolate
²/₃ cup shortening
2 cups sugar
4 eggs
1 teaspoon vanilla
1¼ cups all-purpose flour
1 teaspoon baking powder
1 teaspoon salt
1 cup chopped nuts, if desired
Glossy Chocolate Frosting (below)

Heat oven to 350°. Grease baking pan, 13 × 9 × 2 inches. Heat chocolate and shortening in 3-quart saucepan over low heat until melted; remove from heat. Stir in sugar, eggs and vanilla. Mix in remaining ingredients. Spread in pan. Bake until brownies begin to pull away from sides of pan, about 30 minutes. (Do not overbake.) Cool slightly; spread with Glossy Chocolate Frosting, if desired. Cool completely; cut into bars, about 2 × 1½ inches.

GLOSSY CHOCOLATE FROSTING

3 ounces unsweetened
  chocolate
3 tablespoons shortening
2 cups powdered sugar
¼ teaspoon salt
⅓ cup milk
1 teaspoon vanilla
½ cup finely chopped nuts, if desired

Heat chocolate and shortening over low heat until melted. Stir in powdered sugar, salt, milk and vanilla; beat until smooth. Place pan of frosting in bowl of ice and water; continue beating until smooth and of spreading consistency. Stir in nuts.

Oatmeal Brownies

2 1/2 cups oats
3/4 cup all-purpose flour
3/4 cup packed brown sugar
1/2 teaspoon baking soda
3/4 cup margarine or butter, melted
Brownies (page 62)

Heat oven to 350°. Grease baking pan, 13 × 9 × 2 inches. Mix oats, flour, brown sugar and baking soda; stir in margarine. Reserve 3/4 cup of the oatmeal mixture. Press remaining oatmeal mixture in pan. Bake 10 minutes; cool 5 minutes.

Prepare Brownies as directed except omit nuts. Spread dough over baked layer. Sprinkle with reserved oatmeal mixture. Bake until brownies begin to pull away from sides of pan, about 30 minutes. (Do not overbake.) Cool; cut into about 1 1/2-inch squares.

Mousse Brownies

1/2 cup margarine or butter
1 package (12 ounces) semisweet
  chocolate chips
1 2/3 cups sugar
1 1/4 cups all-purpose flour
1 teaspoon vanilla
1/2 teaspoon baking powder
1/2 teaspoon salt
3 eggs
1 cup chopped nuts
Mousse Topping (below)

Heat oven to 350°. Grease rectangular pan, 13 × 9 × 2 inches. Heat margarine and chocolate chips in 3-quart saucepan over low heat, stirring constantly, until melted. Stir in remaining ingredients except nuts and Mousse Topping until smooth; stir in nuts, if desired. Spread in pan.

Prepare Mousse Topping; pour evenly over batter. Bake 45 minutes; cool 2 hours. Cut into 1 1/2- or 2-inch squares.

MOUSSE TOPPING

3/4 cup whipping cream
1 package (6 ounces) semisweet chocolate
  chips
3 eggs
1/3 cup sugar
1/8 teaspoon salt

Heat whipping cream and chocolate chips in 2-quart saucepan, stirring constantly, until chocolate is melted and mixture is smooth; cool slightly. Beat remaining ingredients until foamy; stir into chocolate mixture.

Marbled Brownies

Cream Cheese Filling (below)
1 cup margarine or butter
4 ounces unsweetened chocolate
2 cups sugar
4 eggs
2 teaspoons vanilla
1 1/2 cups all-purpose flour
1/2 teaspoon salt
1 cup coarsely chopped nuts

Heat oven to 350°. Prepare Cream Cheese Filling. Heat margarine and chocolate over low heat until melted; cool. Beat chocolate mixture, sugar, eggs and vanilla in large mixer bowl on medium speed, scraping bowl occasionally, about 1 minute. Beat in flour and salt on low speed, scraping bowl occasionally, about 30 seconds. Beat on medium speed about 1 minute. Stir in nuts.

Spread half of the batter in greased baking pan, 9 × 9 × 2 inches. Spread with Cream Cheese Filling. Lightly spread remaining batter over Cream Cheese Filling. Gently swirl through batter with spoon in an over-and-under motion for marbled effect. Bake until wooden pick inserted in center comes out clean, 55 to 65 minutes; cool. Cut into bars, 2 × 1 inch.

CREAM CHEESE FILLING

1 package (8 ounces) cream cheese, softened
1/4 cup sugar
1 teaspoon ground cinnamon
1 egg
1 1/2 teaspoons vanilla

Beat all ingredients in small mixer bowl, scraping bowl occasionally, about 2 minutes.

Almond Brownies

2/3 cup shortening
4 ounces unsweetened chocolate
2 cups sugar
1 1/4 cups all-purpose flour
1 cup chopped almonds
1 cup chopped almond paste
1 teaspoon baking powder
1 teaspoon salt
4 eggs

Heat oven to 350°. Heat shortening and chocolate in 3-quart saucepan over low heat until melted; remove from heat. Stir in remaining ingredients. Spread in greased rectangular pan, 13 × 9 × 2 inches.

Bake until brownies begin to pull away from sides of pan, about 30 minutes. Do not overbake. Cool slightly. Cut into bars, about 2 × 1 1/2 inches.

Double-Frosted Brownies

Deluxe Brownies (page 68)
1 1/2 cups powdered sugar
1/2 cup whipping cream
1/3 cup margarine or butter
1 teaspoon vanilla
3 ounces unsweetened chocolate, melted
  and cooled

Prepare Deluxe Brownies; cool. Heat powdered sugar, whipping cream and margarine to boiling in 2-quart saucepan over medium heat, stirring constantly. Boil, without stirring, until candy thermometer registers 234° or until small amount of mixture dropped into very cold water forms a soft ball that flattens when removed from water; cool slightly. Beat in vanilla until mixture is smooth and of spreading consistency; spread over brownies. Spread chocolate over frosting. Refrigerate until chocolate is set. (Refrigerate until 1 hour before serving in warm weather.) Cut into 1-inch squares.

Following pages: Marbled Brownies, Double-frosted Brownies and Mousse Brownies

Deluxe Brownies

16 BROWNIES

2/3 cup margarine or butter
5 ounces unsweetened chocolate, cut into pieces
1 3/4 cups sugar
2 teaspoons vanilla
3 eggs
1 cup all-purpose flour
1 cup chopped nuts

Heat oven to 350°. Heat margarine and chocolate over low heat, stirring constantly, until melted; cool slightly. Beat sugar, vanilla and eggs on high speed 5 minutes. Beat in chocolate mixture on low speed. Beat in flour just until blended. Stir in nuts. Spread in greased square pan, 9 × 9 × 2 inches.

Bake just until brownies begin to pull away from sides of pan, 40 to 45 minutes; cool. Cut into about 2-inch squares.

Butterscotch Brownies

18 BROWNIES

1/4 cup shortening or vegetable oil
1 cup packed brown sugar
1 egg
1 teaspoon vanilla
3/4 cup all-purpose or whole wheat flour
1 teaspoon baking powder
1/2 teaspoon salt
1/2 cup chopped nuts

Heat oven to 350°. Heat shortening over low heat until melted; remove from heat. Mix in brown sugar, egg and vanilla. Stir in remaining ingredients. Spread in greased baking pan, 8 × 8 × 2 inches. Bake 25 minutes. Cut into 1 3/4-inch squares while warm.

BRAZIL NUT BROWNIES: Substitute 3/4 cup ground Brazil nuts for the chopped nuts.

BUTTERSCOTCH-DATE BROWNIES: Decrease vanilla to 1/2 teaspoon. Stir in 1/2 cup snipped dates with the remaining ingredients.

COCONUT-BUTTERSCOTCH BROWNIES: Decrease vanilla to 1/2 teaspoon. Substitute shredded coconut for the nuts.

DELICATE COOKIES

Russian Teacakes

ABOUT 4 DOZEN COOKIES

1 cup margarine or butter, softened
1/2 cup powdered sugar
1 teaspoon vanilla
2 1/4 cups all-purpose or whole wheat flour
1/4 teaspoon salt
3/4 cup finely chopped nuts
Powdered or colored sugar

Heat oven to 400°. Mix margarine, 1/2 cup powdered sugar and the vanilla. Stir in flour, salt and nuts. Shape dough into 1-inch balls. Place on ungreased cookie sheet. Bake until set but not brown, 8 to 9 minutes. Roll in powdered sugar while warm; cool. Roll in powdered sugar again.

AMBROSIA BALLS: Substitute 1 cup shredded coconut and 1 tablespoon grated orange peel for the nuts.

SURPRISE CANDY TEACAKES: Decrease nuts to 1/2 cup. Cut 12 vanilla caramels into fourths or cut 1 bar (4 ounces) sweet cooking chocolate into 1/2-inch squares. Shape dough around pieces of caramel or chocolate to form 1-inch balls.

Following pages: Florentines

French Lace Crisps

²/₃ cup packed brown sugar
¹/₂ cup light corn syrup
¹/₂ cup shortening
1 cup all-purpose flour
1 cup finely chopped nuts

Heat oven to 375°. Heat brown sugar, corn syrup and shortening to boiling over medium heat, stirring constantly; remove from heat. Stir in flour and nuts gradually. Keep batter warm over hot water. Drop by teaspoonfuls about 3 inches apart onto lightly greased cookie sheet. Bake only 8 or 9 cookies at a time. Bake until set, about 5 minutes. Let stand 3 to 5 minutes; remove from cookie sheet.

Little Wreaths

1 cup sugar
³/₄ cup margarine or butter, softened
³/₄ cup shortening
2 teaspoons grated orange peel
2 eggs
4 cups all-purpose flour
1 egg white
2 tablespoons sugar
Red candied cherries
Green candied citron

Heat oven to 400°. Mix 1 cup sugar, the margarine, shortening, orange peel and eggs. Stir in flour. Shape dough by rounded teaspoonfuls into ropes, about 6 inches long. Form each rope into circle, crossing ends and tucking under. (This shaping method is easier than the traditional method of tying knots.) Place on ungreased cookie sheet. Beat egg white and 2 tablespoons sugar until foamy; brush over tops of cookies. Press bits of candied cherries on center crisscross for holly berries; add little jagged leaves cut from citron. Bake until set but not brown, 10 to 12 minutes. Remove immediately from cookie sheet.

Crisp Fried Cookies

10 egg yolks
1/3 cup powdered sugar
1/2 cup whipping cream
1 tablespoon Cognac or other brandy
1 teaspoon ground cardamom
1/2 teaspoon grated lemon peel
2 to 2 1/2 cups all-purpose flour
Vegetable oil
Powdered sugar

Beat egg yolks and 1/3 cup powdered sugar until very thick and lemon colored, about 10 minutes. Stir in cream, Cognac, cardamom and lemon peel. Mix in enough flour to make stiff dough. Cover and refrigerate at least 3 hours.

Heat oil (2 inches) in small deep saucepan to 375°. Divide dough into halves. Roll each half 1/16 to 1/8 inch thick on well-floured board. Cut dough into 4 × 2-inch diamonds with pastry wheel or knife. Make 1-inch crosswise slit in center of each; draw long point of diamond through slit and curl back in opposite direction. Fry until delicate brown, about 15 seconds on each side; drain on paper towels. Store in airtight container. Just before serving, sprinkle with powdered sugar.

Florentines

1/4 cup sugar
3/4 cup whipping cream
1/4 cup all-purpose flour
1/2 cup slivered almonds, very finely chopped
8 ounces candied orange peel, very finely chopped
2 bars (4 ounces each) sweet cooking chocolate, cut into pieces

Heat oven to 350°. Blend sugar and cream. Stir in flour, almonds and orange peel. (Mixture will be thin.) Drop by teaspoonfuls onto heavily greased and floured cookie sheet. Spread mixture into thin circles with knife or spatula.

Bake just until edges are light brown, 10 to 12 minutes. Let cool a few minutes before removing from cookie sheet; cool. Melt chocolate over low heat, stirring constantly, until melted. Turn cookies upside down; spread with chocolate. Let stand at room temperature until chocolate is firm, at least 3 hours. Store in covered container at room temperature or refrigerate.

Following pages: Crisp Fried Cookies

· 8 ·

MOLDED COOKIES

Snickerdoodles

1 1/2 cups sugar
1/2 cup margarine or butter, softened
1/2 cup shortening
2 eggs
2 3/4 cups all-purpose flour
2 teaspoons cream of tartar
1 teaspoon baking soda
1/4 teaspoon salt
2 tablespoons sugar
2 teaspoons ground cinnamon

Heat oven to 400°. Mix 1 1/2 cups sugar, the margarine, shortening and eggs. Stir in flour, cream of tartar, baking soda and salt. Mold dough by rounded teaspoonfuls into balls. Mix 2 tablespoons sugar and the cinnamon; roll balls in mixture to coat. Place about 2 inches apart on ungreased cookie sheet. Bake until set, 8 to 10 minutes. Remove immediately from cookie sheet.

Lemon-Ginger Crinkles

1 cup packed brown sugar
1/2 cup shortening
1 egg
1 tablespoon grated lemon peel
1 1/2 cups all-purpose flour
1/2 teaspoon baking soda
1/2 teaspoon cream of tartar
1/4 teaspoon salt
1/4 teaspoon ground ginger
Granulated sugar

Heat oven to 350°. Mix brown sugar, shortening, egg and lemon peel. Stir in flour, baking soda, cream of tartar, salt and ginger. Mold dough into 1-inch balls; dip tops in granulated sugar. Place on ungreased cookie sheet. Bake until almost no indentation remains when touched, 10 to 11 minutes.

Farm-style Oatmeal Cookies

2 cups packed brown sugar
1 cup lard or shortening
1/2 cup buttermilk
1 teaspoon vanilla
4 cups quick-cooking oats
1 3/4 cups all-purpose or whole wheat
    flour
1 teaspoon baking soda
3/4 teaspoon salt

Heat oven to 375°. Mix brown sugar, lard, buttermilk and vanilla. Stir in remaining ingredients. Mold dough into 1-inch balls. Place about 3 inches apart on ungreased cookie sheet. Flatten with bottom of glass dipped in water. Bake until golden brown, 8 to 10 minutes. Remove immediately from cookie sheet.

Thumbprint Cookies

1/4 cup packed brown sugar
1/4 cup margarine or butter, softened
1/4 cup shortening
1 egg, separated
1/2 teaspoon vanilla
1 cup all-purpose or whole wheat flour
1/4 teaspoon salt
3/4 cup finely chopped nuts
Jelly

Heat oven to 350°. Mix brown sugar, margarine, shortening, egg yolk and vanilla. Stir in flour and salt. Mold dough into 1-inch balls. Beat egg white slightly. Dip balls into egg white; roll in nuts. Place about 1 inch apart on ungreased cookie sheet; press thumb deeply in center of each. Bake until light brown, about 10 minutes. Remove immediately from cookie sheet; cool. Fill thumbprints with jelly.

Following pages: Thumbprint Cookies and Farm-style Oatmeal Cookies

Peanut Butter Cookies

¹/₂ cup granulated sugar
¹/₂ cup packed brown sugar
¹/₄ cup margarine or butter, softened
¹/₄ cup shortening
¹/₂ cup peanut butter
1 egg
*1 ¹/₄ cups all-purpose or whole wheat
    flour*
³/₄ teaspoon baking soda
¹/₂ teaspoon baking powder
¹/₄ teaspoon salt

Mix sugars, margarine, shortening, peanut butter and egg. Stir in remaining ingredients. Cover and refrigerate at least 3 hours.

Heat oven to 375°. Mold dough into 1¹/₄-inch balls. Place about 3 inches apart on ungreased cookie sheet. Flatten in crisscross pattern with fork dipped in flour. Bake until light brown, 9 to 10 minutes. Cool 2 minutes; remove from cookie sheet.

INVISIBLE-MINT COOKIES: For each cookie, mold 1 level tablespoonful dough around chocolate mint wafer. Place on lightly greased cookie sheet. Sprinkle tops with finely chopped peanuts or chocolate shot. Bake until set but not hard, 10 to 12 minutes.

Raisin Crisscross Cookies

³/₄ cup sugar
¹/₄ cup margarine or butter, softened
¹/₄ cup shortening
1 egg
¹/₂ teaspoon lemon extract
1 ³/₄ cups all-purpose flour
³/₄ teaspoon cream of tartar
³/₄ teaspoon baking soda
¹/₄ teaspoon salt
1 cup raisins

Heat oven to 400°. Mix sugar, margarine, shortening, egg and lemon extract. Stir in remaining ingredients. Mold dough by rounded teaspoonfuls into balls. Place about 3 inches apart on ungreased cookie sheet. Flatten in crisscross pattern with fork dipped in flour. Bake until light brown, 8 to 10 minutes.

CHOCOLATE CRISSCROSS COOKIES: Substitute ¹/₂ cup semisweet chocolate chips for the raisins.

Peanut Butter–Chocolate Kisses

½ cup granulated sugar
½ cup packed brown sugar
½ cup creamy peanut butter
¼ cup margarine or butter, softened
¼ cup shortening
1 egg
1½ cups all-purpose flour
¾ teaspoon baking soda
½ teaspoon baking powder
Granulated sugar
About 3 dozen milk chocolate candy
   kisses or stars or desired amount
   chocolate-coated peanut candies

Heat oven to 375°. Mix ½ cup granulated sugar, the brown sugar, peanut butter, margarine, shortening and egg thoroughly. Stir in flour, baking soda and baking powder. Mold dough into 1-inch balls; roll in sugar. Place about 2 inches apart on ungreased cookie sheet. Bake until edges are light brown, 8 to 10 minutes. Immediately press candy kiss firmly in each cookie; cool.

Raspberry Jam Strips

1 cup margarine or butter, softened
½ cup granulated sugar
½ cup packed brown sugar
1 egg
1 teaspoon vanilla
2½ cups all-purpose flour
1 teaspoon baking powder
½ cup raspberry jam
Almond Glaze (below)

Mix margarine, sugars, egg and vanilla. Stir in flour and baking powder. (If dough is soft, cover and refrigerate at least 1 hour.)

Heat oven to 350°. Divide dough into 8 equal parts. Mold each part into strip, 8 × 1½ inches, on ungreased cookie sheet. Make slight indentation down center of each with handle of wooden spoon; fill with about 1½ teaspoons jam. Bake until edges are light brown, 10 to 12 minutes. Cool slightly. Drizzle with Almond Glaze. Cut diagonally into 1-inch pieces.

ALMOND GLAZE

1 cup powdered sugar
½ teaspoon almond extract
2 to 3 teaspoons water

Beat powdered sugar, almond extract and water until smooth and of desired consistency.

Greek Easter Cookies

1 cup margarine or butter, softened
⅓ cup granulated sugar
2 egg yolks
1 teaspoon vanilla
½ teaspoon brandy flavoring
2 cups all-purpose flour
1 teaspoon baking powder
1 teaspoon ground cloves
Powdered sugar

Heat oven to 350°. Mix margarine, granulated sugar, egg yolks, vanilla and, if desired, brandy flavoring. Stir in flour, baking powder and cloves. Mold dough into ¾-inch balls or 2-inch-long crescents. Place on ungreased cookie sheet. Bake until set but not brown, 8 to 10 minutes. Cool 2 minutes; remove from cookie sheet. Cool completely; roll in powdered sugar.

Gingersnaps

1 cup sugar
¾ cup shortening
¼ cup dark molasses
1 egg
2¼ cups all-purpose flour
1½ teaspoons baking soda
1 tablespoon ground ginger
1 teaspoon ground cinnamon
¼ teaspoon salt
Sugar

Mix 1 cup sugar, the shortening, molasses and egg. Stir in flour, baking soda, ginger, cinnamon and salt. Cover and refrigerate at least 1 hour.

Heat oven to 375°. Mold dough by rounded teaspoonfuls into balls; dip tops in sugar. Place balls, sugared sides up, about 3 inches apart on lightly greased cookie sheet. Bake until edges are set (centers will be soft), 10 to 12 minutes. Remove immediately from cookie sheet.

Bonbon Cookies

3/4 cup powdered sugar
1/2 cup margarine or butter, softened
1 tablespoon vanilla
Few drops food color
1 1/2 cups all-purpose flour
1/8 teaspoon salt
Dates, nuts, semisweet chocolate chips,
    candied cherries or maraschino
    cherries
Vanilla Glaze or Chocolate Glaze (below)

Heat oven to 350°. Mix powdered sugar, margarine, vanilla and, if desired, food color. Work in flour and salt until dough holds together. (If dough is dry, mix in 1 to 2 tablespoons milk.) For each cookie, mold dough by tablespoonful around date, nut, chocolate chips or cherry to form ball. Place about 1 inch apart on ungreased cookie sheet. Bake until set but not brown, 12 to 15 minutes; cool. Dip tops of cookies into Vanilla Glaze. Decorate with coconut, nuts, colored sugar, chocolate chips or chocolate shot if desired.

VANILLA GLAZE

1 cup powdered sugar
1 tablespoon plus 1 1/2 teaspoons milk
1 teaspoon vanilla

Beat powdered sugar, milk and vanilla until smooth and of desired consistency. Tint parts of glaze with different food colors, if desired.

CHOCOLATE GLAZE

1 cup powdered sugar
2 tablespoons milk
1 ounce unsweetened chocolate,
    melted and cooled
1 teaspoon vanilla

Beat powdered sugar, milk, chocolate and vanilla until smooth and of desired consistency.

BROWN SUGAR–BONBON COOKIES: Substitute 1/2 cup packed brown sugar for the powdered sugar. Omit food color.

CHOCOLATE-BONBON COOKIES: Omit food color. Stir 1 ounce melted unsweetened chocolate (cool) into margarine mixture.

Acorn Cookies

1 cup sugar
1 cup margarine or butter, softened
1/2 cup milk
1 teaspoon vanilla
1 teaspoon almond extract
1 egg
3 1/2 cups all-purpose flour
1 teaspoon baking powder
1/4 teaspoon salt
1 package (12 ounces) semisweet
    chocolate chips
2 cups finely chopped nuts

Mix sugar, margarine, milk, vanilla, almond extract and egg. Stir in flour, baking powder and salt. Cover and refrigerate at least 4 hours.

Heat oven to 375°. For each cookie, mold 1 tablespoon dough into 2-inch oval. Taper one end by pinching dough. Place about 1 inch apart on ungreased cookie sheet. Bake until set and very light brown, 9 to 12 minutes. Remove immediately from cookie sheet; cool.

Heat chocolate chips until melted. Dip about 1/3 of the wide, rounded end of each cookie into chocolate, then dip into nuts.

CHOCOLATE-NUT LOGS: For each cookie, mold 1 teaspoon dough into 2 1/2-inch rope. Bake as directed. Dip ends of cookies into chocolate; dip into nuts. Makes about 8 dozen cookies.

PEPPERMINT CANDY CANES: Substitute 1 teaspoon peppermint extract for the almond extract. Divide dough into halves. Add 1/2 teaspoon red food color to 1 half of dough. For each candy cane, mold 1 teaspoon dough from each half into 4-inch rope by rolling back and forth on floured surface. Place 1 red and 1 white rope side by side; press together lightly and twist. Place on ungreased cookie sheet; curve top of cookie down to form handle of cane. Bake as directed. Mix 2 tablespoons finely crushed peppermint candy and 2 tablespoons sugar. Immediately sprinkle over baked cookies. Makes about 4 1/2 dozen cookies.

Crisp Pastel Cookies

¾ cup shortening (part margarine or
   butter, softened)
½ cup sugar
1 package (3 ounces) fruit-flavored
   gelatin
2 eggs
1 teaspoon vanilla
2½ cups all-purpose flour
1 teaspoon baking powder
1 teaspoon salt

Heat oven to 400°. Mix shortening, sugar, gelatin, eggs and vanilla. Stir in remaining ingredients. Mold dough into ¾-inch balls. Place about 3 inches apart on ungreased cookie sheet. Flatten with bottom of glass dipped in sugar. Bake 6 to 8 minutes.

Hidden Chocolate Cookies

½ cup granulated sugar
¼ cup packed brown sugar
¼ cup margarine or butter, softened
¼ cup shortening
1 egg
½ teaspoon vanilla
1⅔ cups all-purpose flour
½ teaspoon baking soda
¼ teaspoon salt
About 30 chocolate mint wafers

Heat oven to 400°. Mix sugars, margarine, shortening, egg and vanilla. Stir in flour, baking soda and salt. Mold about 1 tablespoonful dough around each wafer. Place about 2 inches apart on ungreased cookie sheet. Bake until light brown, 9 to 10 minutes.

· 9 ·

REFRIGERATOR AND PRESSED COOKIES

Old-fashioned Refrigerator Cookies

ABOUT 5 DOZEN COOKIES

1 cup packed brown sugar
1 cup margarine or butter, melted
1 egg
1 teaspoon vanilla
3 cups all-purpose flour
1 1/2 teaspoons ground cinnamon
1/2 teaspoon baking soda
1/2 teaspoon salt
1/3 cup chopped nuts
Glaze (below)

GLAZE

2 cups powdered sugar
1/4 cup milk

Mix brown sugar, margarine, egg and vanilla. Stir in flour, cinnamon, baking soda, salt and nuts. Shape dough into 2 rectangles, 5 × 3 × 1 1/2 inches. Refrigerate until firm, about 2 hours.

Heat oven to 375°. Cut dough into 1/8-inch slices. Place about 2 inches apart on ungreased cookie sheet. Bake until light brown, 6 to 8 minutes. Cool; drizzle with Glaze.

Mix powdered sugar and milk until smooth. Stir in 2 to 3 tablespoons additional milk, if necessary.

Lemon Cookie Sandwiches

1/2 cup sugar
1/2 cup margarine or butter, softened
1 tablespoon water
1 teaspoon vanilla
2 eggs, separated
1 1/2 cups all-purpose flour
1/2 teaspoon salt
1/4 teaspoon baking soda
2/3 cup finely chopped nuts
Lemon Filling (below)

Mix sugar, margarine, water, vanilla and egg yolks. Stir in flour, salt and baking soda. Divide dough into halves. Shape each half into roll, about 1 1/2 inches in diameter and about 7 inches long. Wrap and refrigerate at least 4 hours.

Heat oven to 400°. Cut rolls into 1/8-inch slices. Place about 1 inch apart on ungreased cookie sheet. Beat egg whites slightly; stir in nuts. Spoon 1/2 teaspoon nut mixture onto half of the cookie slices. Bake until edges begin to brown, about 6 minutes. Remove immediately from cookie sheet; cool. Put nut-topped and plain cookies together in pairs with Lemon Filling, placing the nut-topped cookies on top.

LEMON FILLING

1 cup powdered sugar
2 teaspoons margarine or butter, softened
1 teaspoon grated lemon peel
1 tablespoon plus 1 1/2 teaspoons lemon
  juice

Beat all ingredients until smooth.

Vanilla Cookie Slices

1 cup sugar
1 cup margarine or butter, softened
2 eggs
1 1/2 teaspoons vanilla
3 cups all-purpose flour
1 teaspoon salt
1/2 teaspoon baking soda

Mix sugar, margarine, eggs and vanilla. Stir in remaining ingredients. Divide into 3 equal parts. Shape each part into roll, about 1 1/2 inches in diameter. Wrap and refrigerate at least 4 hours but no longer than 6 weeks.

Heat oven to 400°. Cut rolls into 1/8-inch slices. Place about 1 inch apart on ungreased cookie sheet. Bake 8 to 10 minutes. Remove immediately from cookie sheet.

BUTTERSCOTCH SLICES: Substitute packed brown sugar for the granulated sugar.

CHRISTMAS TREES: Divide dough into halves. Shape into 3 rolls, each 14 inches long, using 1/2 of the dough for the largest roll, 2/3 of the second half for the medium roll and the remaining dough for the smallest roll. Coat rolls with green sugar. Wrap and refrigerate. Heat oven to 400°. Cut each roll into 1/4-inch slices. Place about 1 inch apart on ungreased cookie sheet. Bake until edges are delicate brown, 8 to 10 minutes; cool. Stack 3 slices, from largest to smallest, spreading Easy Frosting (below) between each. Top each tree with red cinnamon candy dipped in frosting. Makes about 4 1/2 dozen cookies.

EASY FROSTING

1 cup powdered sugar
1/4 teaspoon salt
1/2 teaspoon vanilla
1 tablespoon plus 1 1/2 teaspoons milk
* or 1 tablespoon water*

Beat powdered sugar, salt, vanilla and milk or water until smooth and of spreading consistency.

SHAMROCKS: Tint dough with green food color. Divide into 4 equal parts. Shape each part into roll, about 1 inch in diameter. Coat rolls with green sugar. Wrap and refrigerate. Heat oven to 400°. Cut rolls into $\frac{1}{8}$-inch slices. For each cookie, place 3 slices, with sides touching, on ungreased cookie sheet; press sides together. Attach stem cut from another slice. Bake about 7 minutes. Makes about 6 dozen cookies.

CINNAMON SLICES: Substitute $\frac{1}{2}$ cup packed brown sugar for $\frac{1}{2}$ cup of the granulated sugar and 1 tablespoon ground cinnamon for the vanilla.

COOKIE TARTS: Spoon 1 teaspoon jelly or preserves onto half of the slices; top with remaining slices. Seal edges. Cut slits in tops so filling shows. Makes about $3\frac{1}{2}$ dozen tarts.

ORANGE-ALMOND SLICES: Mix in 1 tablespoon grated orange peel with the margarine and $\frac{1}{2}$ cup cut-up blanched almonds with the flour.

PEANUT BUTTER SLICES: Substitute packed dark brown sugar for the granulated sugar and $\frac{1}{2}$ cup crunchy peanut butter for $\frac{1}{2}$ cup of the softened margarine.

WALNUT SLICES: Stir in $\frac{1}{2}$ cup chopped black walnuts.

WHOLE WHEAT SLICES: Substitute whole wheat flour for the all-purpose flour.

Following pages: Vanilla Cookies: Cinnamon, Vanilla, Walnut, Orange-Almond and Shamrocks

Date-Nut Pinwheels

ABOUT 5 DOZEN COOKIES

12 ounces pitted dates, cut up
1/3 cup granulated sugar
1/3 cup water
1/2 cup chopped nuts
1 cup packed brown sugar
1/4 cup margarine or butter, softened
1/4 cup shortening
1 egg
1/2 teaspoon vanilla
1 3/4 cups all-purpose flour
1/4 teaspoon salt

Cook dates, granulated sugar and water in saucepan, stirring constantly, until slightly thickened; remove from heat. Stir in nuts; cool.

Mix brown sugar, margarine, shortening, egg and vanilla until smooth. Stir in flour and salt. Divide into halves. Roll each half into rectangle, about 11 × 7 inches, on waxed paper. Spread half of the date-nut filling over each rectangle. Roll up tightly, beginning at 11-inch side. Pinch edge of dough to seal well. Wrap and refrigerate at least 4 hours but no longer than 6 weeks.

Heat oven to 400°. Cut rolls into 1/4-inch slices. Place about 1 inch apart on ungreased cookie sheet. Bake until light brown, about 10 minutes. Remove immediately from cookie sheet.

Spritz

ABOUT 5 DOZEN COOKIES

1 cup margarine or butter, softened
1/2 cup sugar
2 1/4 cups all-purpose flour
1 teaspoon almond extract or vanilla
1/2 teaspoon salt
1 egg

Heat oven to 400°. Mix margarine and sugar. Stir in remaining ingredients. Fill cookie press with dough; form desired shapes on ungreased cookie sheet. Bake until set but not brown, 6 to 9 minutes.

CHOCOLATE SPRITZ: Stir 2 ounces unsweetened chocolate, melted and cooled, into margarine mixture.

Antoinettes

Spritz dough (page 92)
Raspberry preserves
Rich Chocolate Frosting (below)

Heat oven to 400°. Prepare dough as directed for Spritz. Fill cookie press with dough. Using wide fluted plate on cookie press, form long strips of dough on ungreased cookie sheet. Cut into 2-inch lengths. Bake until set but not brown, 6 to 9 minutes. Immediately remove from cookie sheet. Just before serving, spread flat side of half of the cookies with raspberry preserves. Top with remaining cookies. Frost tops with Rich Chocolate Frosting.

RICH CHOCOLATE FROSTING

2 tablespoons shortening
1 square (1 ounce) unsweetened chocolate
1 cup powdered sugar
2 tablespoons boiling water

Heat shortening and chocolate over low heat until melted; remove from heat. Stir in powdered sugar and boiling water. Beat in few drops hot water, if necessary, until smooth and of spreading consistency.

Orange Crisps

½ cup granulated sugar
½ cup packed brown sugar
½ cup margarine or butter, softened
½ cup shortening
2½ cups all-purpose flour
1 egg
2 teaspoons grated orange peel
1 tablespoon orange juice
¼ teaspoon baking soda
¼ teaspoon salt

Heat oven to 375°. Mix sugars, margarine and shortening. Stir in remaining ingredients. (If dough is too stiff, add egg yolk. If dough is not stiff enough, add small amounts of flour.) Fill cookie press with dough; form desired shapes on ungreased cookie sheet. Bake until light brown, 8 to 10 minutes.

LEMON CRISPS: Substitute lemon peel and juice for the orange peel and juice.

Following pages: Viennese Shortbread

Lemon-Cheese Cookies

1 cup sugar
1 cup margarine or butter, softened
1 package (3 ounces) cream cheese,
    softened
1 egg
1 teaspoon grated lemon peel
1 tablespoon lemon juice
2 1/2 cups all-purpose flour
1 teaspoon baking powder

Mix sugar, margarine, cream cheese, egg, lemon peel and lemon juice. Stir in flour and baking powder. Cover and refrigerate at least 30 minutes.

Heat oven to 375°. Fill cookie press with dough; form desired shapes on ungreased cookie sheet. Bake until light brown, 8 to 9 minutes.

CHOCOLATE-CHEESE COOKIES: Omit lemon peel and lemon juice. Stir 2 ounces melted unsweetened chocolate (cool) into margarine mixture.

Viennese Shortbread

1 cup margarine or butter, softened
1/2 cup powdered sugar
1/2 teaspoon vanilla
2 cups all-purpose flour
1/4 teaspoon baking powder
Mocha Filling (below)

Heat oven to 375°. Mix margarine, powdered sugar and vanilla. Stir in flour and baking powder. Fill cookie press with dough. Using medium star plate on cookie press, form 3-inch strips of dough on ungreased cookie sheet. Bake until edges are light brown, 7 to 9 minutes; cool. Put cookies together in pairs with Mocha Filling. For fancier cookies, dip edges in melted sweet chocolate, if desired.

MOCHA FILLING

1 teaspoon powdered instant coffee
1 teaspoon boiling water
2/3 cup powdered sugar
2 tablespoons margarine or butter,
    softened

Mix instant coffee and water until coffee is dissolved. Mix in powdered sugar and margarine. Stir in few drops water, if necessary.

RED SPOON TIPS

The introduction to this collection of Betty Crocker's best recipes provides the fundamental information needed to bake delicious cookies with prize-winning results. Red Spoon Tips goes even further by offering advice on ingredients and their substitutions, baking equipment and much more. Read on for hints that will help you bake cookies better and more professionally than ever before.

Decorating Cookies

Some plain cookies look their best that way. More often than not, though, cookies lend themselves to decoration. Sometimes the question "to decorate or not" is answered by a lack of time. But decorating cookies doesn't have to be a time-consuming project. It depends on the sort of decorating involved, and even then decorating usually takes less time than one might think.

The fun of decorating is letting your imagination roam. Many of the cookies in this book are accompanied by frosting or icing suggestions. The possibilities that go on from there are endless.

Listed below are just a few of those possibilities:

- Sprinkle frosted or iced cookies with chopped nuts. Press the nuts into the topping while it is still wet; that way, the nuts will hold fast to the cookie.
- Arrange raisins, currants or candied cherry halves or cherry cut-outs on pale-frosted cookies before the frosting or icing sets.
- Drizzle melted chocolate (unsweetened chocolate, for continental sophistication) in abstract patterns over the tops of cookies. This is a great, easy way to dress up frosted or iced bar cookies.
- Dark-colored or chocolate-frosted cookies benefit from drizzled glazes, too. You can use any of the thinner powdered sugar glazes and even tint the glazes with food coloring if you like.
- A sprinkling of sifted, powdered sugar is often enough to "dress" a plain cookie, whether dark or light. For large plain cookies that aren't very pale, center a paper doily over the cookie before sifting the sugar; then, carefully remove the doily, leaving a sugar design.

- Press cinnamon candies into cookie-dough cut-outs before baking. Although the candies soften with heating, they don't melt enough to spread. The design you make with the candies will be unchanged when the cookies come out of the oven.
- Nonpareils (tiny, multicolored round candies) add charming specks of bright color. Press them into the tops of unbaked cookies or scatter them over frosting or icing before it sets. Stir 1 to 2 tablespoons nonpareils into sugar cookie dough for simple rolled cookies with a starburst of color shot throughout.
- Christmas cookies just wouldn't be the same without red- and green-colored sugars. Dust unbaked cookies with sugar or sprinkle it over frosted or iced cookies.
- Jimmies, sprinkles and chocolate shots are colorful ways to decorate unbaked or frosted cookies without any fuss—just sprinkle!
- Pipe icing with the help of a pastry bag. Twists, shells, lettering, flowers, leaves and more are at your fingertips. If you want to pipe simple lines (as for lettering) but don't have a pastry bag, you can make a piping "cone" from a simple letter envelope: Put about 1/3 cup of icing in one corner of an envelope; fold the envelope sides toward the center. Snip off just the corner to make a tip. The more the corner is snipped away, the thicker the piping will be.
- Turn rolled cookies into hanging ornaments. Use a drinking straw to poke a hole in the dough at the top of the cookie before baking. When the baked cookie has cooled, slip a length of yarn through the hole.

Giving Cookies

Cookies make wonderful gifts. If you can set aside one dozen cookies in the freezer each time you bake, you will soon have a delightful selection for gift-giving. It is advisable to package cookies so that they will stay fresh and not be liable to break. Before packing cookies into a gift cookie tin (or any other covered container, for that matter), make sure that the lid fits snugly. Cushion the cookies with sheets of waxed paper, plastic wrap or aluminum foil between layers, and crunch bright tissue paper around them to keep them from breaking when the tin or container is jostled.

When packing cookies into a basket or bag, remember that they won't last unless they are properly covered. Cookies that don't have gooey toppings may be individually wrapped. Ziplock-style plastic bags of all sizes are superb for keeping air out and crumbs in. If you plan to give several kinds of cookies at one time, place the frosted or more fragile ones on top. Again, pack crushed colored tissue paper around the layers to cushion them. Then, just tie up your package with some pretty ribbon and you have the perfect gift.

Cookie Tips

TIPS FOR BAR COOKIES: Use the pan size called for in the recipe. If you don't have the correct size pan, choose a different type of cookie to bake. Make sure that the cookie dough is spread to the sides and right into the corners of the pan. If you are not sure when the cookies are done, insert a wooden pick into the center of the pan. If it comes out wet, they need more time. Let bar cookies cool completely in the pan unless the recipe directs otherwise.

TIPS FOR ROLLED COOKIES: Roll only part of the dough at a time and keep the remainder refrigerated. For easiest handling, use a well-floured rolling pin cover (sometimes called a "stockinette" or "sock") and board cover. Roll out the dough with light, even pressure. If dough sticks to your cookie cutters, dip them in flour and wipe off any accumulated dough as you go along. Cut cookies close together so you don't have to roll the dough out more times than necessary (that makes cookie dough tough). Lift cut-out cookie dough with a spatula; it's the easiest way to transfer it to the cookie sheet.

TIPS FOR DROP COOKIES: Use an ordinary, tableware teaspoon to scoop up dough. If the dough is especially sticky, use a second teaspoon to push the dough off the first spoon onto the cookie sheet. Don't crowd the dough on the cookie sheet. The recipe will instruct you as to how far apart the dough should be placed.

TIPS FOR MOLDED COOKIES: Make all of the cookies the same size, so that they will bake evenly. Work with small amounts, keeping the remaining dough refrigerated. If the dough is still too soft, mix in 1 to 2 tablespoons flour. If the dough is too dry and crumbly, work in 1 to 2 tablespoons milk, water, or softened margarine or butter. Place dough on a thoroughly cooled cookie sheet (the cookies will spread on a warm one, and that will spoil all your careful work). If a recipe recommends flattening the cookies, use the bottom of a glass dipped in flour or sugar, or press down with a fork.

TIPS FOR REFRIGERATOR COOKIES: Shape the dough into a smooth roll of the recommended diameter. Chill the dough as the recipe directs. If it hasn't been chilled properly, it won't be firm enough to slice easily. Take only as much dough as you need to work with out of the refrigerator at one time. Keep the refrigerated dough tightly wrapped in waxed paper, plastic wrap or aluminum foil and twist the ends to seal. Use a sharp, thin-bladed knife for slicing the dough.

TIPS FOR PRESSED COOKIES: Chill the dough only if specified in the recipe. Test the dough for consistency before adding all the flour. Put a small amount of dough into the cookie press and squeeze out one or two "test" cookies. The dough should be soft and pliable, but not crumbly. If the dough seems too stiff, mix in 1 egg yolk; if it seems too soft, mix in 1 to 2 tablespoons flour. Hold the press so that it rests on the cool cookie sheet (unless you are using a star or bar plate). Raise the press as soon as enough dough has been released to form a cookie. If using a star or bar plate, hold the press slightly above the cookie sheet.

Keeping Cookies on Hand: The Freezer

Managing to keep cookies around the house isn't always easy. To keep them from disappearing *too* quickly, or to keep some stored away for future occasions, the freezer is the answer. All kinds of cookies freeze well, and in the end it pays to freeze them rather than to let them sit at room temperature for weeks.

Frosted cookies can be frozen for 2 to 3 months. As soon as they are cooled and frosted, arrange them in a single layer on a baking sheet and set the sheet, uncovered, in the freezer. When the cookies are firm, pack them in a single layer in an airtight container lined with plastic wrap or aluminum foil. Seal the lining, close the container and label it clearly, including the date. (If freezing both frosted and unfrosted cookies in the same container, abide by the shorter freezing time for frosted cookies.)

Unfrosted cookies can be frozen for 9 to 12 months. Arrange thoroughly cooled cookies as above, separating single layers of cookies with sheets of waxed paper, aluminum foil or plastic wrap. Then seal the lining, close and label the container as directed above.

Frozen cookies thaw very quickly. Arrange them in a single layer on a serving plate and let them stand, uncovered, at room temperature for 15 to 20 minutes.

To store rolls of refrigerated cookie dough, wrap airtight in plastic wrap and freeze. The frozen dough will keep for 5 to 6 months, and there's a bonus: Because the frozen dough holds its shape even better than chilled dough, it is easier to slice into smooth, uniform disks.

Mailing Cookies

Choose any of the Cookies That Travel Well from the list on page 101. If you want to send rolled cookies, cut the cookies into rounded shapes rather than shapes with points that will break easily. The smaller the cookie, the less likely it is to crumble or snap.

For extra protection in mailing, cut cookies only slightly smaller in circumference than a soup or fruit juice can. Then, wrap the cookies "back to back" in pairs and ease them into the can. Or, wrap cookies singly or in pairs and pack them in large, resealable coffee or shortening cans, shoe or clothing boxes, or gift boxes or tins.

When packing cookies, fill the space around them with torn paper, packing foam or plastic bubble-wrap. Give the package a gentle shake to make sure the cookies don't move back and forth. Pad the top with added packing.

Pack the containers in sturdy packing boxes (foil-lined corrugated cardboard or fiberboard are best). Stuff packing materials around the containers to pad them.

Seal the packing box with waterproof tape, wrap in heavy brown paper, seal with tape and tie with a strong cord.

Write the address in legible print directly on the package or on a mailing label. Cover the address with transparent tape to protect it from smudging; do the same with the return address.

All-Time Favorite Cookies

COOKIES THAT TRAVEL WELL

- Applesauce-Spice Drops
- Candy Cookies
- Chocolate Chip Cookies
- Double Chocolate Oatmeal Cookies
- Lemon-Ginger Crinkles
- Mexican Cookies
- Peanut Butter Cookies
- Salted Peanut Crisps
- Snowflake Molasses Cookies
- Sour Cream Drops

COOKIES IN A HURRY

- Candy Cookies
- Chocolate Chip Cookies
- Date-Nut Squares
- Granola-Plum Bars
- Oatmeal Cookies

- Scotch Shortbread
- Toffee Bars

OLD-FASHIONED COOKIES

- Farm-style Oatmeal Cookies
- Fruit-filled Drops
- Gingersnaps
- Lemon-Ginger Crinkles
- Raisin Crisscross Cookies
- Snickerdoodles
- Vanilla Cookie Slices

COOKIES THAT CAN BE MADE WITH WHOLE WHEAT FLOUR

- Butterscotch Brownies
- Chocolate Drops
- Crisp Ginger Cookies
- Date Bars
- Ginger Creams
- Lemon Squares
- Mixed Nut Squares
- Peanut Butter Cookies
- Russian Teacakes
- Soft Pumpkin Drops
- Sugar Cookies
- Thumbprint Cookies
- Whole Wheat Slices

KIDS' FAVORITE COOKIES

- Gingerbread Boys and Girls
- Handprint Cookies

CHRISTMAS COOKIES

- Christmas Trees
- Gingerbread Boys and Girls
- Light Ginger Cookies
- Little Wreaths
- Peppermint Candy Canes
- Russian Teacakes
- Snowflake Molasses Cookies

EASY COOKIES FOR BEGINNING BAKERS

- Butterscotch Brownies
- Date-Nut Squares
- Crisp Pastel Cookies
- Easy Praline Bars
- Farm-style Oatmeal Cookies
- Russian Teacakes
- Spritz Cookies

Ingredients Used in This Book

The baker will benefit from a brief introduction to some of the ingredients used in the recipes in this book.

ALMOND PASTE: Use almond paste, not marzipan. It can be somewhat crumbly or grainy but should be moist enough to hold together when pressed into a ball.

BAKING POWDER: Use double-action baking powder.

BUTTER: In baking, butter should be used at room temperature unless the recipe directs otherwise. If you must proceed with a recipe before the butter has warmed to room temperature, cut it into small pieces (or grate it, using the side of the grater with the largest holes); it will warm up quickly. Do not use "whipped" butter, as it has air pumped into it.

Butter should be stored, tightly covered, in the refrigerator, where it will keep for at least 2 weeks. If you are uncertain of its freshness, taste it; you will easily be able to tell if it is "off," unless it has been heavily salted. Unsalted butter contains less water and, of course, less salt. Keep it well wrapped, or it will pick up odors from nearby foods. Butter can be stored in the freezer.

CHOCOLATE: To melt chocolate, break it into small pieces (if it is not in pieces already). Place in a heatproof bowl or in the top of a double boiler set over very hot—not boiling—water. Stir occasionally while the chocolate melts. The microwave oven is a wonderful tool for melting chocolate, too. Stir at the minimum melting time; remember that chocolate can hold its shape even when it is almost melted. We use the following chocolate when baking cookies:

- *Semisweet Chocolate Chips:* These chocolate chips are sold in bags of 6 and 12 ounces.
- *Sweet Cooking Chocolate:* This is often labeled "sweet baking chocolate" and packaged in 8-ounce bars.
- *Unsweetened Chocolate:* Do not confuse "dark" or "bitter" chocolate with un-

sweetened chocolate; they contain considerable amounts of sugar. Unsweetened chocolate is conveniently available in paper-wrapped, 1-ounce squares.

CITRON: This fruit is a relative of the lemon and resembles the quince in appearance. It has a very thick skin, and in the United States that is the portion of the fruit we use. What is meant by "citron" here is citron peel that has been chopped, brined, cooked and then candied.

COCOA: This is unsweetened cocoa powder and is not to be confused with the instant cocoa or hot chocolate mixes.

COCONUT: Sweetened coconut is best when packaged in airtight bags and cans. Whether you buy coconut flaked (small bits) or shredded (thicker, longer strands), it should be moist.

CORN SYRUP: Corn syrup makes for somewhat elastic, easy-to-handle doughs. "Light" corn syrup is specified in recipes where the deeper flavor of "dark" corn syrup would be overbearing. If neither "light" nor "dark" is specified, either one may be used.

CREAM CHEESE: To soften cream cheese, allow it to come to room temperature. Beat it vigorously until it is smooth and creamy. Do not substitute "whipped" cream cheese.

CURRANTS: The dried form of fresh currant berries is known as "currants," too. Currants have a tendency to become as dry and hard as peppercorns once the box they're packaged in has been opened and closed a number of times. To rejuvenate dry currants, cover them with hot water and allow them to stand for 10 to 15 minutes, then drain them. To soften and flavor them at the same time, cover them with brandy, rum or sherry (or any liqueur that tickles your fancy) instead of water; it isn't necessary to warm the alcohol.

EGGS: The recipes in this book were tested with large eggs. Buy eggs with clean, uncracked shells. Kept in the refrigerator, eggs do not actually spoil for weeks; they do, however, lose moisture and flavor as time goes by. Separated yolks or whites can be kept in tightly covered containers in the refrigerator for 2 to 4 days. For unbroken yolks add enough cold water to the container they are in to cover them.

FLOUR: These recipes were developed with all-purpose flour. Recipes in which whole wheat flour can be substituted with success are indicated. (See page 101 for a comprehensive list of those recipes.) Cookies made with stone-ground flour may spread more and have a coarser texture than those made with regular whole wheat flour.

GRATED ORANGE, LEMON OR LIME PEEL: Wash the fruit well and pat it dry. Grate on the side of the grater with the smallest holes and stop grating when you can see the bitter white pith. For easy cleanup, set the grater over a sheet of waxed paper.

LARD: Much used in early American cookery, lard has been upstaged in recent years by vegetable shortening. Lard gives some baked goods an old-fashioned flavor. Try Farm-style Oatmeal Cookies (page 77). In baking, lard is used at room temperature.

MARGARINE: Margarine is less expensive than butter and lower in cholesterol. If you don't expect it to taste like butter on its own, you won't be disappointed. In cookies, it can be hard to taste the difference between butter and margarine. Use margarine at room temperature. It will keep, refrigerated, for about 1 month.

MILK: Whole, skim or reconstituted, nonfat dry milk can be stored in the refrigerator for 5 to 7 days. Other kinds of milk used in baking:

- *Buttermilk:* This is the liquid that remains after butter has been churned. Buttermilk can be kept refrigerated for about 2 weeks.
- *Evaporated Milk:* This rich milk is sold in cans and is shelf-stable until opened, after which time it must be refrigerated.
- *Sweetened Condensed Milk:* This canned milk adds richness and sweetness in one step. Like evaporated milk, it is shelf-stable until opened and then it must be refrigerated.

MOLASSES: The flavor of molasses, a by-product of sugar refining, can vary. A recipe will specify if "dark" or "light" molasses is preferred. If only "molasses" is called for, it will not make a difference which is used.

NUTS: When nuts are called for, you may use any sort of nuts you like. Some recipes indicate that they are best with particular nuts, such as almonds, black walnuts, Brazil nuts, cashews, peanuts, pecans, salted mixed nuts and walnuts. A number of cookies are made with blanched (skinned) almonds. You can buy blanched almonds (whole, halved, slivered or chopped). If you don't mind the extra effort you can blanch whole almonds yourself. Simply cover the almonds with boiling water and let sit for 10 minutes. Drain, cover with cold water, and let sit several minutes longer. The skins should slip off easily.

Nuts keep well in airtight packages, especially when refrigerated. But they don't keep indefinitely, so taste nuts before you add them to the dough; you don't want a rancid nut in your cookie.

OATS: If a recipe does not specify "quick-cooking" as opposed to "regular" oats, using one rather than the other will not strongly affect the finished cookies. However, do not substitute "instant oatmeal."

RAISINS: We use dark, seedless raisins. To plump raisins that seem very dry, follow the procedure for softening currants.

SHORTENING: Use a solid, hydrogenated, un-flavored vegetable fat that is available in 1- and 3-pound cans. Do not substitute vegetable oil.

SOUR CREAM: We specify "dairy" sour cream. Do not substitute artificial sour cream or sour cream substitutes.

SUGAR: Use granulated sugar where simply "sugar" is called for. In addition to plain, granulated sugar, we use:

- *Brown Sugar:* When we call for "brown sugar," either "light" or "dark" is fine. We do specify where the stronger flavor of dark brown sugar is preferred. When measuring brown sugar, pack it down firmly in the measuring cup.
- *Powdered Sugar:* This is known also as "10X sugar" and "confectioners' sugar." Do not sift powdered sugar before measuring it, unless it is extremely lumpy.

VARIETY BAKING MIX: This dry, all-purpose baking mix is used for quick breads, main dishes and desserts and includes flour, buttermilk and leavening.

VEGETABLE OIL: Choose a vegetable oil with a light, unobtrusive flavor. Do not substitute oil for butter, margarine, lard or shortening, whether solid or melted. Oil will make the dough too soft.

VINEGAR: Use white distilled vinegar or cider vinegar.

Equipment for Baking Cookies

Baking cookies calls for some basic kitchen tools. Here is a brief list of essential items:

GRADUATED MEASURING CUPS: These cups are usually sold in nests. Always use the proper cup size to measure the quantity needed.

GLASS (LIQUID) MEASURING CUPS: These transparent measures are commonly found in 8-, 16- and 32-ounce sizes.

GRADUATED MEASURING SPOONS: Spoons that are broad and shallow, rather than round and deep, are sometimes easier to use for dipping directly into packages with shallow openings.

COOKIE SHEETS: Cookie sheets have only one or two rims so that hot air can circulate freely around the cookies. Remember that shiny, heavy-gauge aluminum sheets are best for cookies; those with a dark finish tend to overbrown the bottoms of cookies.

SPATULA OR PANCAKE TURNER: A metal spatula is flexible and thin enough to slip easily under the most fragile cookies.

COOLING RACKS: To avoid soggy cookies, choose sturdy metal racks that stand well above any kitchen surface.

BAKING PANS: The recipes in this book call for pans in four sizes only: a 15½ × 10½ × 1-inch jelly roll pan, a rectangular 13 × 9 × 2-inch pan, and square pans 9 × 9 × 2 inches and 8 × 8 × 2 inches.

ROLLING PIN: Whether wooden or metal, a rolling pin is indispensable to any lover of rolled cookies.

It should go without saying that you will need a selection of **mixing bowls** (both small and large bowls), a sturdy **rubber scraper** and an **electric mixer** or **wooden spoon** for mixing batter. Additional equipment that is nice to have:

- *Sifter:* Although a fine mesh sieve can be used to sift lumpy powdered sugar and the like, a sifter is neater.
- *Grater or zester:* Either of these will grate citrus peel quickly and efficiently. If nei-

ther is available, use a vegetable peeler to pare thin strips of peel (avoid the bitter white pith), then mince the peel with a sharp knife as finely as possible.

- *Cookie cutters:* Of course cookie dough can be cut freehand, but cookie cutters are much more fun.
- *Oven timer:* If you set your oven timer every time a cookie sheet goes into the oven, you will never wind up with a batch of burned cookies.
- *Cookie press:* Several models of press are available, all with an assortment of disks. Change disks to change the shape of the cookies.
- *Pastry bag:* With so many different tips to choose from, pastry bags are versatile decorating tools. To pipe icing without a pastry bag, see page 98 for instructions on making an envelope cone.

Table of Equivalents

Here are some equivalent measurements of ingredients commonly used in baking.

Apricots	1 pound	3 cups
Baking chocolate, unsweeted	8 ounces	8 squares
Cherries, maraschino	10-ounce jar	33 cherries
Chocolate chips	6 ounces	1 cup
Coconut, shredded or flaked	4 ounces	1$\frac{1}{3}$ cups
Cranberries, fresh	1 pound	4 cups
Cream cheese	8 ounces	1 cup
	3 ounces	6 tablespoons
Dates, pitted and cut up	1 pound	2$\frac{1}{2}$ cups
Figs, dried and cut up	1 pound	2$\frac{2}{3}$ cups
Flour		
all-purpose	1 pound	3$\frac{1}{2}$ cups
whole wheat	1 pound	3$\frac{1}{3}$ cups
Lemon juice	1 medium lemon	2 to 3 tablespoons
Lemon peel, grated	1 medium lemon	1$\frac{1}{2}$ to 3 teaspoons
Margarine (or other shortening)	1 pound	2 cups
Milk, sweetened condensed	14 ounces	1$\frac{1}{3}$ cups
Nuts, shelled		
almonds	1 pound	3$\frac{1}{2}$ cups
peanuts	1 pound	3 cups
pecans	1 pound	4 cups
walnuts	1 pound	6$\frac{1}{4}$ cups
Orange peel, grated	1 medium orange	1 to 2 tablespoons
Prunes, dried, whole, pitted	1 pound	2$\frac{1}{4}$ cups
Raisins	1 pound	2$\frac{3}{4}$ cups
Sour cream	8 ounces	1 cup
Sugar		
brown (packed)	1 pound	2$\frac{1}{4}$ cups
granulated	1 pound	2 cups
powdered	1 pound	4 cups
Variety baking mix	60-ounce package	13 cups

Emergency Substitutions

An emergency is the only excuse for using a substitute ingredient. Results will vary. In a pinch you can make the following adjustments:

INGREDIENT	SUBSTITUTE
1 whole egg	2 egg yolks + 1 tablespoon water
1 cup fresh whole milk	½ cup evaporated milk + ½ cup water or 1 cup reconstituted nonfat dry milk + 2 teaspoons margarine or butter
1 ounce unsweetened chocolate	3 tablespoons cocoa + 1 tablespoon margarine or butter
1 cup honey	1¼ cups sugar + ¼ cup liquid

INDEX

Credits

V.P., Associate Publisher: Anne M. Zeman
Project Editor: Rebecca W. Atwater
Creative Director: J.C. Suarès
Photographer: Anthony Johnson
Designer: Patricia Fabricant
Production Editor: Kimberly Ebert

112